International Bus...

CULTURAL SOURCEBOOK AND CASE STUDIES

LINDA B. CATLIN
Wayne State University

THOMAS F. WHITE
The University of Colorado at Denver

COLLEGE DIVISION South-Western Publishing Co.

Cincinnati Ohio

Acquisitions Editor: Randy G. Haubner
Production Editor: Rebecca Roby
Production House: Bookmark
Cover Design: Craig LaGesse Ramsdell
Cover Illustration: © 1993 Bob Hambly
Internal Design: Russell Schneck Design
Photo Researcher: Kathryn A. Russell
Senior Marketing Manager: Scott D. Person

1 2 3 4 5 6 7 8 9 0 D1 2 1 0 9 8 7 6 5 4 3

Printed in the United States of America

Library of Congress Cataloging-in-Publication Data

Catlin, Linda B.,
    International business: cultural sourcebook and case studies/
Linda B. Catlin, Thomas F. White.
    p.   cm.
    ISBN 0-538-83518-4
    1. International trade—Cross-cultural studies. 2. International business
    enterprises—Cross-cultural studies. I. White, Thomas F.,   II. Title.
HF1379.C378 1994
658.8'48—dc20   93-31480
                                                                            CIP

I (T) P South-Western is a subsidiary of ITP (International Thomson Publishing). The trademark ITP is used under license.

PREFACE

During the last several years, American business schools have initiated changes in their curricula that reflect the globalization of markets and the changing role of business practitioners in a rapidly evolving international environment. Many courses now have an international component; textbooks include examples of doing business abroad; and international business courses are among the required courses. These changes represent a first and important step in preparing students to function effectively in today's American companies.

This book of original, cross-cultural case studies and exercises is designed to assist instructors with the second step of the process. Written by a marketing practitioner and instructor and by a cultural anthropologist, the book offers students and instructors the unique perspectives of both business administration and cultural anthropology on doing business internationally. And as one corporate president, whose company manufactures industrial equipment for American and European businesses, told the authors, "University students have to be international in their outlook. If they're not, they might as well jump into a cocoon and let it seal over them. The comfort of doing just what we want to do is gone. The world is too small, communication is too rapid."

The *Sourcebook* will help students develop this international outlook. It is intended to supplement textbooks in junior, senior, and MBA-level courses in marketing, management, organizational behavior, and international business. The case studies and exercises provide a framework within which students must apply and integrate, in a specific cultural setting, some of the principles they learn in these courses. Moreover, the activities provide an opportunity for students to work in groups to analyze situations and formulate strategies, much as they will do in the "real world" of international business.

Although each case or exercise involves a specific culture—such as that of Japan, Australia, France, Puerto Rico, or Germany—none is intended to teach students everything they need to know about that particular culture. Rather, the goal is to convey some of the issues and concerns students need to be aware of when dealing with other cultures, and to suggest the importance of studying in-depth the culture, history, politics, and geography of an area. These cases and exercises suggest many of the *questions* to ask about the unfamiliar, and they provide some—but not all—of the answers.

The volume is titled a "sourcebook" because it includes a number of features that students and instructors can use to heighten their cross-cultural skills and awareness, not just within the context of a particular course, but in their personal and professional lives as well. In addition to the cases and exercises, the book has several other features:

- ■ To introduce students to case study analyses, the authors include a short case study with questions for students to answer. A sample student response and the instructor's critique of the student's answers provide a guide for what is expected in this sort of analysis.

- ■ The Instructor's Manual contains additional exercises that can be used at the beginning of or during the semester to introduce students to concepts such as ethnocentrism and the role cultural values play in the workplace.

- ■ Articles from various business journals accompany several of the cases. These articles were selected because they provide specific background information for the case, as well as general information about the topics covered in the case.

- The Suggested Readings at the end of each section in the Instructor's Manual and the student text, plus the Bibliography at the end of the text, provide a listing of academic and practice-oriented materials that should prove useful beyond the semester in which students use this textbook supplement. Also, they can be used as the starting point for a term project if the instructor assigns one.

- The compendium of foreign films is intended to provide a list of high-quality films that elucidate some aspect(s) of another culture. They provide an additional, pleasurable method for students to use in learning about how people in other cultures cope with the exigencies of life, how they relate to each other at work and in personal relationships, and how they delineate the parameters of their particular worldview.

- The Glossary contains definitions of the unusual terms used in the case studies and exercises, plus some of the more common words that have a specific connotation within the context of this book.

The material in this book covers many of the potential problem areas international managers, and domestic managers who work with different ethnic groups, must deal with; these include human resource issues, financial and economic situations that cause stress, and consumer behavior in new and unfamiliar environments. The primary goal of the case studies and exercises is to teach students how to work effectively and comfortably with individuals who may not share the same belief systems, values, or communication styles.

Acknowledgments

The genesis of this book was written with the assistance of a grant from the Dean's Office, College of Liberal Arts, and the Department of Anthropology at Wayne State University. Marietta L. Baba, Professor in the Business and Industrial Anthropology sequence at Wayne State, supported this project at its inception and we thank her for her encouragement.

Several business administration and anthropology instructors have helped the authors field test portions of this material during its development. We especially appreciate the cooperation of Nils-Erik Aaby and Greg Prang in letting us use their classrooms as a laboratory for this purpose.

This book of cross-cultural case studies and exercises derives much of its usefulness and relevance from the knowledge, insights, and experience that numerous business practitioners have shared with the authors. Many individuals have helped us in the preparation of this book and the authors gratefully acknowledge their contribution.

In the United States, we must acknowledge the assistance of Pat and Bruce Allen, Grant Bibby, Roy and Edith Bowers, Anita Dobin, Dennis Farhat, Rufina Geskin, Herb Gurzinski, Lauren Krohn, Jim Lehner, Paul Maruyama, Nancy Negohosian, David Sell, Hugh Sofy, Janet Sofy, and Brad Thompson.

Managers and experts from other countries who graciously contributed their perspectives and their time include James Caller (Great Britain), Les Coleman (Australia), Michael Dennehy (Ireland), Hans-Andreas Fein (Germany), Leonardo Ffrench (Mexico), and Kazuko Sawano (Japan).

Finally, we wish to thank our students who over the years have shown an interest in and given suggestions for a book that would help to expand their knowledge of the global marketplace. We hope that this volume helps them and other students to achieve their goals in the international realm.

CONTENTS

ANALYZING
CASE STUDIES

STEPS IN ANALYZING A CASE STUDY

Case study analysis is an important skill for all business practitioners. It is a skill you will use in many of your university business classes, and in whatever professional position you hold in an organization. In the cases you will be reviewing in this textbook, the facts are given to you in a "package," that is, most—but not necessarily all—of the information you need is presented in a few paragraphs. When you are faced with similar problems in your job, you will need to prepare a similar "package" of facts before you can analyze and make recommendations about the situation. Each case study in this book has a list of "Suggested Readings" that will give you some additional facts and ideas you can use in analyzing the case study.

Outlined below are the general steps which you should follow when analyzing a case study in class, as well as in your work environment. (Some of the case studies in this book will give you specific instructions and questions to answer that differ from or are in addition to the steps listed below.)

1. Identify all *pertinent facts* in the case.
   a. Look for important information that is given in the case study and important information that is *missing* from the case, including trends in the business environment.
   b. Develop location maps, floor plans, timelines, organizational charts, and other visual aids from the information presented in the case to help you gain a better understanding of the case.
   c. If tables of data or charts are given in the case, look for exceptional cases or trends.

2. Formulate a *problem statement* or *question* that summarizes the central issue of the case.
   a. Distinguish between *symptoms* and *underlying problems*.
   b. Don't be misled by opinions expressed in the case.

3. Identify *resources* and *weaknesses* that pertain to the problem.

4. Create alternative courses of action.

5. Choose *one course of action* for your recommendation and state your reasoning for choosing it.

In the following section you will find a case study entitled "The Düsseldorf Trade Show." Read the case and prepare your own analysis using the outline above, plus the specific questions at the end of the text. Then, compare your analysis with the "Student Analysis" that follows the case. Finally, compare both these analyses with the "Critique" written by an instructor.

SAMPLE CASE STUDY FOR ANALYSIS: THE DÜSSELDORF TRADE SHOW

Brown Automation Company, located in Davenport, Iowa, manufactures transfer presses for the automotive and appliance industries. The company employs 125 people and has annual sales of $11 million. Currently, company representatives are making plans to participate in a large manufacturing trade show in Düsseldorf, Germany.

During the last three years, Brown's sales department has received from European and Japanese firms numerous telephone and written requests for information about the company's products. Several of these firms have called back after receiving the Brown sales literature and asked that a Brown representative contact the foreign firm when the representative visits Europe or Japan. Until now, Brown has never sent anyone outside North America on sales trips or to attend trade shows, although the company has sold its equipment to several Canadian firms.

Earlier this year, the company president, Jim Nelson, decided that the company should participate in the Düsseldorf show. His decision was based on two considerations: first, domestic sales are down 15 percent due to cutbacks in the automotive industry; and second, the increasing number of requests for information from foreign firms convinced him that there was a large potential market in Europe for Brown's products. Jim began preparing for the trade show by calling together Tom Messaic, marketing manager; John Harper, engineering manager; and Alex Carrero, controller.

This group of managers first interviewed two American consultants who had worked with other American companies in setting up marketing operations in Europe, including Germany, and who had contacts throughout Europe in several industries. When the Brown trade show team discussed the pros and cons of hiring one of these consultants to manage the company's participation in the Düsseldorf trade show, Tom and John were in favor while Jim and Alex argued that the $15,000 fees were too high. As Jim said, "We've participated in many shows here in the United States and shows can't be that much different in Germany. I know my managers can handle the Düsseldorf show on their own. Tom, I want you to take charge of this one, and, John, I want you to work closely with him to cover the technical aspects related to equipment."

Tom began his preparations by calling a meeting of his staff. His marketing coordinator, Janice Beacon, suggested that they contact the local university to find someone who was familiar with German culture.

"When I studied in France during my junior year in college, I found some big differences between the way we do things here and the way the French do those same things," she said. "I think we need to be aware of how Germans conduct business differently than Americans do."

"I'm sure you're right, Janice," Tom replied, "but right now I think we need to concentrate on some of the technical details of putting together this trade show in Germany. Remember, we've only got four months to figure out how to get our equipment there, what the booth will look like, and whom we'll send to staff the booth. And Alex has given us a pretty small budget to do all this, so we need to be careful about how we spend the money."

"I've drawn up a list of our usual planning areas for trade shows," Tom continued. "And I've assigned each one of you to take charge of one or two of these areas. I'd like you to put together a plan for covering these at the Düsseldorf show. We'll meet again in two weeks to go over what you've done. Thanks for your input today."

Tom assigned responsibility for the following list of trade show areas to members of his staff:

- Publications, including sales and technical literature for the company's equipment, information about the firm, and business cards
- Staffing requirements for the booth and the hospitality suite at the nearby hotel
- The physical setup of the booth, including size, equipment displays, and backdrop
- Promotional items and giveaways for business people visiting the booth

Instructions. Assume that you are Tom Messaic, marketing manager for Brown Automation.

1. What issues and questions should your staff members bring up for each of the areas associated with the trade show in Düsseldorf? What are the details that need to be decided on in each area?

2. What special considerations are necessary since this trade show is in Germany and not in the United States?

3. Based on your answers to these questions, what will you recommend to Mr. Nelson, the company president, regarding Brown's participation in the Düsseldorf show this year?

STUDENT ANALYSIS OF SAMPLE CASE STUDY

In their discussion of what Brown Automation needs to be concerned with in each of the trade show areas, Tom Messaic's assistants should bring up some of the following points:

1. *Publications for the booth:*
   a. Should the sales brochures and technical literature be translated? If so, into which language? Probably the company should have the brochure translated into German since this is the language of the host country. Most people attending the trade show will know English.
   b. Brown Automation may want to print up a piece with general information about the company since it is not well-known in Europe. Company representatives will have their own business cards with them to give out to visitors to the booth.

2. *Staffing the booth:*

   a. The company should probably send its regular sales representatives since they are most familiar with trade shows and with selling the equipment.

   b. The company has to think about whether they need an interpreter for the booth in case some visitors don't speak English. They can hire an interpreter when they get to the show.

3. *Booth setup:*

   a. The first consideration is to decide on what size booth Brown should reserve. They should get a booth similar in size to one they would use at a U.S. trade show, like the one in Chicago. That way the backdrops and display materials they have used at other shows can be used in Düsseldorf, and the equipment will fit in the booth.

   b. Send the usual equipment from the United States to display in the booth so customers can see exactly what Brown equipment looks like.

   c. Europeans use meters and centimeters instead of feet and inches, so signage for the equipment needs to be in meters and centimeters.

4. *Advertising and promotion:* Brown probably has promotional give-aways, for example, printed bags and specialty advertising products, that it uses at U.S. trade shows, and it should take these to give out at the German show.

5. *Recommendation to Jim Nelson, president of Brown Automation:* Go to the trade show in Germany because there is a lot of business to compete for in Europe, and because Brown has a good staff that can put together a good display for the trade show.

INSTRUCTOR'S CRITIQUE OF STUDENT ANALYSIS

The marketing coordinator, Janice Beacon, made an excellent point when she suggested that the company consult a local university person about what might be the differences between doing a trade show in the United States and doing one in Germany. Although there are many similarities between the United States and Germany, there are some subtleties in German business protocol that Americans need to be aware of, even at a trade show.

Students reading and discussing this case will not necessarily come up with answers regarding what Brown Automation should do for all aspects of the trade show. Instead, this case is intended to make students aware of the issues involved in participating in a trade show in a different country.

1. *Publications for the booth:*

a. The student's suggestion that the company brochure be translated into German is a good one. An additional possibility is to keep the English text beside the German text in the new brochure, making it accessible to business people who do not read German but who do read English. Another question is, who should do the translation? Back translation (the process of translating into a second language, then translating back into the original language to check the accuracy of the translation) is a good idea in this instance. A native speaker should be used for this to avoid the incorrect use of slang or idioms.

Also, as the student notes later in the analysis, since the standard measurement unit in Europe is based on the metric system, technical brochures need to include a conversion from inches/feet to centimeters/meters.

b. The information piece about the company should include details about its history, philosophy, and biographical information about the top managers. German business people want to know a lot about the companies and *individuals* with whom they are doing business.

2. *Staffing the booth:*

a. Because executives in European countries place such a high priority on knowing a lot about the companies and *individuals* with whom they are doing business, it might be a good idea to send Brown Automation's top managers to the trade show. If the company decides to send its top managers, should they be from sales, engineering, or both? Because of the technical nature of Brown's products, they probably will want to send managers from both sales and engineering.

b. Even if everyone who visits the booth speaks English, it is a good idea to have an interpreter who can speak one or more European languages as well as English. The student is probably correct in assuming that company representatives will be able to hire an interpreter at the show. However, the average interpreter will have difficulty translating some of the technical terms related to the Brown equipment. This problem can be alleviated by hiring the interpreter the day before the show starts and acquainting him or her with the equipment and the technical terms.

c. The company should also think about what they would recommend as the general deportment for staff members in the booth. A good rule of thumb is, "Act more conservatively than you might at a similar show in the United States." This means conservative business attire (suit and tie), formality in addressing visitors (no first names), and no demonstration of familiarity, such as backslapping or other physical contact except handshakes.

3. *Booth setup:*

   a. A consideration here is, what is considered an average booth size in Germany? Is a 10′ by 10′ too small and likely to make the company look cheap? Is a 20′ by 20′ too large and therefore apt to be regarded as ostentatious? While it would be convenient and economical to use the same backdrops, display materials, and equipment as used in other shows, this may not be the best strategy for a show in Germany. Also, how should the company decorate the booth? Should it be closed or open? What is the generally accepted practice in Germany? The company should request information from the show's management and even pictures from previous shows, if available. Also, ask for the names of American companies attending last year's show and contact them for information.

   b. Getting the equipment to the trade show is a major undertaking. How does the company ensure that it will clear customs smoothly and quickly? Is there a contractor whom the Düsseldorf show manager can recommend?

   c. What do the American exhibitors need to know about working with German trade unions in setting up the show? Can they expect to work with unions in the same way as they do at trade shows in New York, Chicago, and other American cities?

   d. Is there a company that can provide a turn-key operation for the booth setup, thus eliminating the need to ship all the display materials from the United States?

4. *Advertising and promotion:* Are the giveaways used in U.S. shows appropriate for the German audience? Should they be customized for the Düsseldorf show?

5. While this student recommends that the company participate in the trade show, other students may recommend different actions. For example, some may conclude that Brown Automation would be wise to send observers to the Düsseldorf show this year before committing the $40,000–50,000 necessary to participate as an exhibitor. Others may recommend that Mr. Nelson reconsider his decision about using a consultant who has specific knowledge about doing business in Germany. As the marketing department staff has pointed out, there are many differences between doing a trade show in the United States and doing one in Germany; a consultant could help the company deal with these differences more effectively than staff members who are unfamiliar with Germany. A major trade show exposes the company to most of its target market, and a bad first impression may have a high cost.

RELATED EXERCISES AND ACTIVITIES FOR STUDENTS

There are many opportunities in your own community to participate in and learn about business practices and social customs of other cultures. This section contains suggestions for some related cross-cultural exercises and activities to supplement the case studies and exercises in this sourcebook.

1. Attend the traditional wedding ceremony of someone from another culture.

2. Locate the ethnic organizations in your community and obtain their annual calendar of events. Attend a celebration with members of this organization and ask them to explain the significance of the event and the symbolism of the activities.

3. Interview officers of ethnic chambers of commerce, for example, the African-American Chamber of Commerce, Hispanic Chamber of Commerce, and so on.

4. Make an appointment with a representative at a trade mission, consulate, or embassy in your area. Interview this person for information about the business climate in the person's country and determine the feasibility of an American business selling its products there.

5. Interview a representative of the U.S. Department of Commerce who handles trade with one or more foreign countries.

6. Here's a hypothetical situation: Your company wants you to set up a sales office in _____ (choose a country). They want you to research the general cultural issues that the company needs to consider when making a decision about establishing an office there. What sources of information are available to you as you compile this report? (Suggestions: Talk to your reference librarians, look at government documents, interview students from that country, talk to representatives of the country, consult academic specialists on your campus, and so forth.)

7. If you decided you wanted to learn Chinese well enough to do business in China, what resources are available to you in your community?

8. Visit an ethnic restaurant and talk to the proprietor. Ask him or her questions about the business, including:

   ■ Where do you get your specialty ingredients?

   ■ Ask about the unfamiliar foods on the menu.

   ■ What modifications did you have to make in your culture's traditional foods to make them appealing to Americans?

   ■ How closely does your establishment in the United States resemble one that would be found in your native country?

   ■ Is there any cultural significance in the restaurant's decor?

9. Find a foreign-owned firm and interview one of the executives about the company's decision to locate in the United States, how the company prepares or trains employees to work in the United States, and what "surprises" (negative and positive) the company has had since locating in the United States.

10. Find an American company that exports its products. Interview the president or sales manager about how the company made the decision to export and how this decision has affected the company as a whole.

11. The David M. Kennedy Center for International Studies at Brigham Young University publishes a "Culturgram" for most countries of the world. These brief overviews of individual nations include information about the country's customs and courtesies, the people, lifestyle, and demographics.

    Find your library's collection of "Culturgrams" and choose a country about which you know little or nothing. Prepare a short report on the aspects of its religion, demographics, language, and customs that you think would be important to a government agency establishing a trade mission in that country.

CROSS-CULTURAL EXERCISES AND CASE STUDIES

Background Information

Introduction. The next series of exercises involves three situations in which American and Japanese business people must work together to achieve specific business objectives. In each instance, an understanding of the other's business practices, customs, and expectations is essential. The following material will give you a very brief and cursory introduction to some Japanese cultural values. Keep in mind that these values are held in varying degrees by different members of Japanese society. Remember also that a true understanding of any culture requires in-depth study over a long period of time.

Japanese Core Cultural Axioms. Partly because Japan has a fairly homogeneous culture—99.2 percent of its population is Japanese, in contrast to the U.S. population which is very heterogeneous—it is possible to identify several "core cultural axioms." These axioms describe the beliefs of most Japanese; they have evolved over several centuries, and they have a definite impact on the way in which Japanese businesses operate, as well as on other aspects of Japanese life.

Most Japanese scholars identify four core axioms when describing Japanese culture. While a translation for each axiom is given in the description below, there is no idiomatic translation that completely conveys the full meaning of the Japanese term.

Wa—circle. According to the principle of *Wa*, harmony and peace come from loyalty, obedience, and cooperation with other people, including family, peers, and work associates. It is a sacred state that must be maintained.

Amae—oil of life. *Amae* describes (1) the indulgent, dependent love that exists between parents and children, and (2) the total trust between people who are bound by the same obligations, for example, the employee and his supervisor in a work setting. This particular relationship can only exist between two Japanese, never with foreigners (*enryo*).

Tate Shakai—vertical society. In Japanese society, everything is *ranked* and all important relationships are *vertical* rather than *horizontal*. This ranking extends to seniority and titles in a company, to schools and universities (Tokyo University is considered the highest), and to roles in a family.

Giri and *On*. *Giri* comprises the universal obligations one acquires at birth. These obligations extend to ancestors, to parents, and to the nation; they define a role individuals must fulfill during their lifetimes.

On refers to the specific, reciprocal obligations one incurs throughout life. Examples include obligations to teachers and superiors at work.

Business implications. The four core cultural axioms described above have direct and indirect implications for the way the Japanese conduct business, internally and externally.

1. Business objectives include an obligation to the nation, not just to stockholders and management. Moreover, there is a long-term growth orientation with an emphasis on *market share*.

2. There is a close link between government and business—Japan, Inc. The Ministry of International Trade and Industry sets policies and long-term strategies for industry.

3. Companies share some similarities with families. Thirty percent of Japanese companies have lifetime employment, and there is a high degree of loyalty among employees to their companies—60 percent of Japanese workers spend their entire work life in one company, compared to 23 percent in the United States.

4. The seniority system in Japanese companies starts college graduates at the bottom of the corporation; they stay there for about six years and advance together *as a group*, rather than individually as in American companies. Pay in Japanese firms is based more on seniority than on talent, and the personnel department is very important.

5. *Group* competition is encouraged, but not individual competition.

6. Group decision making, the *ringi* system, characterizes the Japanese firm.

7. Unions are company-based, and members work with the company to foster mutual goals.

8. Contracts reflect a long-term commitment and contain little legal language. The latter disrupts *Wa* and suggests an adversarial relationship.

Statistical Comparison of the United States and Japan

	UNITED STATES	*JAPAN*
Founding Date	17th–18th c. A.D.	5th c. A.D.
Land Area	3.6 million sq. mi.	Size of California; 20% arable
Population	240 million	124 million
Population density	26 per square kilometer	322 per square kilometer
Births (per 1000 pop.)	15.5	11.9
Infant mortality	10.0	5.0
People	Pluralistic society; open to immigrants	Homogeneous society; 99.2% Japanese
Natural resources	Abundant	Scarce; must import most resources
Gross domestic product (GDP)	US$4.9 trillion	US$2.9 trillion
Per capita GDP	US$19,815	US$23,325
Exports	US$320 billion	US$260 billion
Imports	US$446 billion	US$165 billion

Sources: Roland Dolan and Robert Worden, eds., *Japan: A Country Study*, 5th ed., Washington, D.C.: Federal Research Division, Library of Congress.

The Economist Book of Vital World Statistics, New York: Random House, 1990.

EXERCISE: AN AMERICAN IN JAPAN

You are the business associates of an American manager who has been hired by a Japanese company. This Japanese company has an office in Seattle, and your associate will be leaving soon to assume the new position there. Your associate knows that he/she will be expected to travel to East Asia on many occasions, to meet with managers at the home office in Tokyo and to talk with suppliers in Singapore. Success in the job depends on being able to work well with the Japanese executives and on establishing congenial relations with the companies in Singapore.

Your associate knows that you have studied business practices in many countries and he/she has asked for your advice about what a person needs to know when working as a foreigner in a Japanese company. While you may not have specific information about Americans working for Japanese companies, or about doing business in Singapore, your knowledge from this course has prepared you to analyze information about other business cultures.

You have decided to counsel your associate about several things in your initial discussion. First, you want to discuss the structure of Japanese companies. Read the article at the end of this section, "American Managers in Japanese Subsidiaries," for ideas to share with your associate. The author of this article outlines some of the cultural differences between American and Japanese managers and discusses how these differences affect American managers in Japanese companies. Draw a graph or chart for the five corporate areas (concept of the firm, concept of a job, authority, management behavior, and human resource management) mentioned in the article and show how the views of many American and Japanese managers differ in these areas.

Second, you want to tell your associate how some Japanese companies view their non-Japanese employees. You found the diagram sketched below in a paper presented at a management conference, and you plan to use it to illustrate your points.

After studying the diagram, answer the following questions:

- How would you explain the meaning of the different circles of this diagram to your associate?

- Why are there two separate circles to represent the same company in Tokyo and in Seattle?

- Who are the "others" represented by the bottom circle?

Third, you want to give your associate some information about Singapore. You know the following facts about Singapore:

- Singapore is a city-state with 238 square miles of territory.

- Its population is 2.5 million.

- The population is divided among several ethnic groups:

  76.6%   Chinese
  14.7%   Malay
   6.4%   Indian
   2.3%   other

- There is close coordination between government and business enterprises to plan the economic system.

- Confucianism is the dominant religion in Singapore, and its tenets emphasize human emotional bonds, group orientation, and harmony.

What does this information suggest to you about doing business with the Singapore suppliers? What recommendations will you give your associate about doing business in Singapore as an employee of a Japanese company?

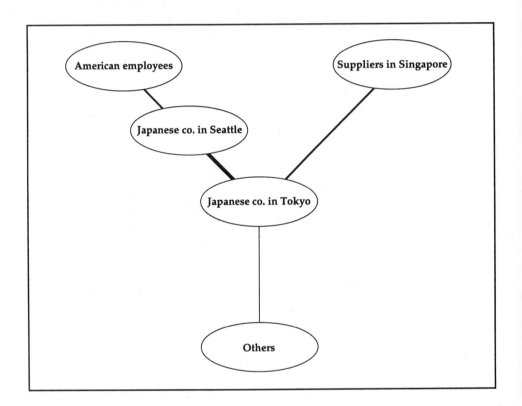

AMERICAN MANAGERS IN JAPANESE SUBSIDIARIES: HOW CULTURAL DIFFERENCES ARE AFFECTING THE WORK PLACE

Mary Sullivan Taylor
Portland State University

Executive Summary

The numbers of Americans working for Japanese firms is rapidly increasing, with an ever growing number of professionals working in these firms. This article explores many of the causes for conflicts that occur between American managers and their Japanese bosses, emphasizing that the root cause is a very different perspective on the purpose of the firm. While for Japanese managers a company exists as much to enhance employee welfare as stockholder welfare, for Americans the firm's goal is to maximize shareholder interest. The ramifications of these differences for such areas as leadership, job description, and interpersonal communication are explored, as are possible solutions to the problems.

By the year 2000, those 250,000 Americans who now work for Japanese firms in the U.S. will see their numbers swell to 1 million. Yet as their numbers grow, so do reports that all is not well with these employees. Disgruntled American executives are filing lawsuits against their employers, claiming breach of promise regarding promotions; enthusiastic U.S. managers who once attempted to meet their bosses halfway by studying Japanese have given up their efforts; American managers claim they are excluded from the real decision-making process, which occurs after they go home. Is this the vaunted Japanese management style that has produced so many books and attempts at imitation?

Reprinted from *Human Resources Planning* with permission of the publisher.

From Blue Collar to White

Before exploring reasons for the increasing number of conflicts between Japanese managers and their American employees, we need first to look at how the composition of the work force within Japanese subsidiaries in the U.S. has changed. Following the wave of manufacturing-plant investments of the late 1970's and early 1980's, Japanese firms in the U.S. have expanded in two new directions: 1) manufacturing plants are adding more American employees in functions such as design and research and development; 2) banking, investment, and trading firms have become more active, extending their services and becoming involved in the mergers and acquisitions usually dominated by U.S. firms. The result is that the number of white-collar employees employed by Japanese firms in the U.S. has increased dramatically in the last few years.

What difference does this make? Simply put, U.S. professionals who work under Japanese managers often find their jobs are now less satisfying. As a gross generalization, while American assembly-line workers have found Japanese management an improvement over conditions under American management, white-collar workers have found conditions worse. When the majority of U.S. employees in Japanese firms worked on the assembly line, reports from the front usually were positive; but, as the balance has shifted toward professional employees, avoidance of dissatisfaction has grown. The reasons lie in how these two cultures define one central concept: Who does the firm exist for? This difference leads to crucial distinctions in job definitions, the concept of leadership, managerial behaviors, the choice of strategic decision makers, and the practice of management development.

To the Japanese, a firm existed as much to provide a livelihood for its employees as to provide a return on assets for stockholders. Job security is not so much a strategic decision as a moral obligation. A manager's duty is thus to look out not only for the bottom line but for the growth of the company—for that is how the firm can ensure employment security and promotion opportunities for its employees.

American managers are not accustomed to this view. Their main responsibility is to achieve short-term profit goals. For U.S. managers, the firm's employees are human resources, assets much like financial capital and technology that are used to attain corporate objectives. They include themselves in the category of human assets and realize that if the company's goals are not achieved—or if the strategic goals change—they may lose their jobs. As a result, American managers tend to see their current position as a stepping stone to higher posts, often in other firms.

Independent Decisions

This difference of perspective leads to a crucial difference between the two groups regarding the concept of a job. American managers expect a job to entail a defined set of duties and responsibilities. Managers expect to be given the authority necessary to carry out their tasks. In a sense, an American manager is like an entrepreneur who is given a certain basket of assets and a clear goal and is rewarded for undertaking individual risk. In addition to the immediate compensation he receives, a manager also gains skills and experience that add to his market value. While this description understates the need for team-player skills and knowledge specific to the firm, it underscores the necessity of clearly delineating the parameters of a job so that the individual's performance can be measured. An American product manager for a biotechnology firm, for example, wants the authority to allocate the marketing budget, decide on the product's message, and choose the outside consultants and advertising agencies she feels are best for the project.

This idea of clear guidelines clashes with that held by Japanese managers. The few job descriptions that exist in Japanese firms usually are ignored. Responsibilities and duties are fluid, often shifting from one person to another within a group as needs and skills demand. The authority for carrying out the group's tasks ultimately rests with the boss. As a consequence, a Japanese manager usually expects his American employees to clear most decisions with him. For example, an American marketing manager who took a business trip he felt was necessary was reprimanded on his return by his Japanese boss for not getting clearance. The American felt the reprimand impugned his ability to make independent decisions; the Japanese manager felt his subordinate had deprived him of important information and that his authority had been undermined.

An American manager's desire for clear job descriptions is, in part, a result of his concern about who is responsible for mistakes, as well as successes. American managers have learned that making errors can lead to being fired. But to their Japanese bosses, this desire to assign blame is irritating. They feel American managers spend more time worrying about who is to blame than concentrating on getting the job done. Most Japanese managers enjoy lifelong job security, so they rarely need to worry about affixing blame for what goes wrong.

Questioning Authority

Although American managers want to know who holds what and how much authority, they display a tendency to question the legitimacy of that authority. In the U.S., a sense of "machismo" comes from defying authority. This creates an interesting paradox: an American manager needs to know how much authority he has, but he constantly is vulnerable to assaults from his subordinates. He survives by developing charisma. American managers rely as much on their personal characteristics as on their position for legitimacy, and their characteristics form the basis of executive leadership.

To understand the Japanese concept of leadership, we need to look at how Japanese managers achieve leadership positions. Japanese managers in the U.S. are products of a system that rewards loyalty and effort with a clear and orderly progression through a hierarchy of authority. Because the firm exists largely for the employees, managers are fairly certain of being retained and allowed to progress. All Japanese managers have been through a fiercely competitive and grueling educational system, and their membership in management ranks is evidence of their survival and competence. Once a manager has proven he has a certain level of ability—by making it through the educational system and into management ranks—he needs only effort (not charisma) to achieve middle management positions.

This fundamental difference in the basis of leadership means that American managers typically exhibit a very different set of behaviors than their Japanese counterparts. To avoid assaults on their authority, they must act confident and knowledgeable—even if they lack both qualities. This attitude is irksome to Japanese managers. The president of a Japanese subsidiary in the Northwest asked, "Why can't young American MBAs exhibit more humility? They are just learning about things, and they should be more modest." An American executive who tries to appear more confident or knowledgeable than he truly is, often is perceived as insincere or dishonest.

How advice and criticism is given and received is another area of conflict between two leadership styles. Japanese managers may be annoyed by subordinates who disagree with them, but they don't feel threatened by such incidents; nor do they feel the need to always appear confident and fully knowledgeable. Knowledge is a resource to be shared, rather than hoarded as a means of maintaining superiority. In Japan, a subordinate can contradict his boss's statement—politely, of course—without fear of retaliation. The Japanese manager feels secure in his position and does not perceive conflicts with employees as tests of his competence. For American managers—instilled with the need to prove their individual worth so they can be rewarded or move on to new jobs—knowledge is a personal asset, and challenges to authority may be perceived as personal threats.

When Japanese and American managers interact in the job setting, these different views of leadership and competency provide the potential for conflict. Japanese managers, who admit when they don't know something, often expect the same behavior from the American managers who work for them. American managers may feel irritated when their Japanese bosses attempt to provide knowledge that contradicts theirs, particularly if the disagreement takes place in front of subordinates.

Try Reasoning First

Closely related to the concept of leadership is management behavior. American managers are keenly aware that, in addition to inspiring confidence through personal charisma, they must interact with their subordinates in a manner that induces workers to stay with the organization. For example, look at how managers ask their subordinates to do certain tasks. The most common tactic used by American managers, according to a survey conducted by Sullivan, Albrecht, and Taylor (in press), is to offer the subordinate reasons why he or she should comply. Failing that strategy, the boss resorts to friendliness. Both tactics reveal a desire to ensure a positive working relationship between manager and employee.

In Japan, managers also prefer reasoning as a compliance strategy. If reasoning doesn't elicit the desired response however, managers will rely on assertiveness—they will simply order the subordinate to do something. Like a military commander giving orders, the Japanese manager in Japan is relieved of the necessity of trying to gain the subordinate's good will, and there are no repercussions for the suspension of civilities. But what happens when the Japanese manager is transferred to the U.S.?

According to a recent study (Sullivan and Taylor, 1989) on compliance-gaining involving managers in Seattle, Portland, and Vancouver, Japanese managers don't seem to change their management style when they come to the U.S. While the survey's sample was small, it suggested that the assertive manner in which Japanese managers ask American professionals to do things is likely to be perceived as brusque or rude, adding to the sense of frustration the American manager already feels from vague job descriptions and mismatch between authority and responsibility. In addition, Japanese managers commonly tell their American subordinates they should comply with a request because it is "for the company." This tactic makes sense if all employees share the view that the company exists as much for them as for the stockholders; but it is not likely to carry much weight with U.S. employees who are unaccustomed to seeing their firm in this light.

The question of trust is another source of frustration for American managers working in Japanese firms. While Japanese executives are prepared to share a great deal of information with their American subordinates, strategic information is guarded more closely. In a study by Pucik, Hanada, and Fifield (1989), Japanese managers indicated they felt wary of sharing such information because the possibility that an American manager will leave for a job at another firm always looms large.

A Great Job, a Poor Career

The differences in American and Japanese cultural perceptions of the firm also affect human resource management practices. As might be expected, Japanese firms in the U.S. offer employees a greater feeling of job security; for that reason, Japanese managers have difficulty accepting employee turnover as a fact of life. In a recent speech to a group of managers in a high-tech firm in Seattle, the president of a Japanese subsidiary in Vancouver commented that he is always asking his American managers to reduce turnover, a request they have trouble understanding since attrition already is low. Management turnover also is lower in Japanese subsidiaries in the U.S. than in comparable U.S. firms; but although American professionals remain with a firm, they criticize their employers for lack of career opportunities and performance appraisals.

In Pucik's (1898) study, a significant proportion of U.S. managers surveyed felt their career advancement opportunities were more limited in a Japanese firm than in an American corporation. There is little management or executive development, they said, and Japanese multinational corporations have more Japanese in the top management ranks of their overseas subsidiaries than comparable U.S. or European firms. Finally, the headquarters of Japanese multinational corporations have remained essentially closed to foreigners. American managers reported that, in a sense, they may have great jobs working in Japanese subsidiaries, but their careers are less than satisfactory.

If U.S. managers find this lack of career opportunity frustrating, they are equally disappointed by their Japanese managers' failure to give performance appraisals. In Japan it is considered as ill-mannered to praise a member of one's family as it would be to praise oneself. Consequently, direct praise is not often heard in a Japanese company, which operates as a kind of family. When a Japanese manager is transferred to the U.S., he finds it hard to give positive feedback to his American subordinates. One American executive who has worked for a Japanese subsidiary for 15 years commented that he has had one performance evaluation in all that time, and has never been told directly that he's doing well.

A Trade-Off?

Given the picture we've painted, it would seem reasonable to expect that American managers would not last long as employees in Japanese subsidiaries. Yet turnover apparently is rather low. Why?

First, it's important to remember that many Japanese subsidiaries have not been in the U.S. long and only recently have started hiring large numbers of white-collar workers. Second, the American manager's sense of greater job security may be overriding his frustrations. Given the period of corporate downsizing that the U.S. has just experienced, job security may be highly attractive. Moreover, American managers in Japanese subsidiaries feel the parent company exhibits great patience and a long-term perspective with regard to such performance goals as profitability. This may be a welcome change from the short-term horizon used in many U.S. firms. And, finally, American managers may find that their Japanese bosses display a more positive attitude toward their mistakes, which allows the Americans to take greater risks.

Even if American managers are not now leaving, they may leave in the future if they're presented with more attractive opportunities for upward mobility in U.S. firms. Given that prospect, Japanese subsidiaries in the U.S. would need to take several steps to avoid increased turnover.

Several recommendations for change by managers can be drawn from the above. These can be grouped into three categories: 1) changes that must be achieved by the top management of the Japanese corporations operating in the U.S.; 2) changes that must be enacted by U.S. managers working in Japanese subsidiaries; and 3) changes required of Japanese managers working in the U.S.

Changes: Top Japanese Management. The first major area requiring change concerns the Japanese corporations themselves. The home offices of Japanese subsidiaries in the U.S. should clarify how they see their overseas subsidiaries—as members of the Japanese corporate family or as foreign contractors. This is a crucial first step. If Japanese corporations expect the same kind of behavior from their U.S. managers as from their Japanese managers, then the same sense of mutual obligation must prevail. It is counterproductive for Japanese top management to profess itself surprised when American managers act in ways that are totally appropriate to the American work scene yet irksome or worse to their Japanese managers. For example, in his book, *Made in America*, Morita (1987) described his shock at being greeted at a trade show by an American who had left Sony American for a better position. To Morita, this man was a traitor, and his friendliness toward him after such "treasonous" behavior was, at first, incomprehensible. Morita's considerable cross-cultural experience eventually led him to understand the appropriateness of this behavior within the American labor scene. Yet the initial shock itself was inappropriate. No Japanese firm in the U.S. should expect its American managers to behave like Japanese managers unless it is willing to treat them in the same way it treats its Japanese work force; that is, to regard them as corporate stakeholders equal in importance to its Japanese employees. (Even then, of course, there are bound to be cultural differences that need to be accommodated.)

Suggestions concerning how the top management of Japanese firms should arrive at a clarification of its philosophy vis à vis foreign employees include 1) retreats where these issues are discussed and clarified and 2) seeking advice from business consultants, both Japanese and foreign. The approach taken probably will depend on the corporation's philosophy and its industry and corporate strategy. Whatever posture is adopted, however, it is important that this policy be clearly communicated to both Japanese and American employees so that behavior (including the decision not to join the firm) can be modified accordingly.

Changes: U.S. Managers. American managers also can contribute toward smoother relationships with their Japanese bosses. One important first step would be to change their expectation concerning the nature of leadership. American managers should expect greater "interference" in their jobs by their Japanese bosses, particularly concerning decisions they may perceive as strictly theirs to make. If the "interference" can be seen as a desire to help, rather than as a negative statement concerning the American manager's competence, it will be easier to accept. In addition, by demonstrating flexibility regarding job and authority boundaries, the American manager

shows he is a "team player" to his Japanese boss—a highly valued trait in Japanese corporate culture.

At the same time, it is important that American managers decrease their expectations regarding feedback on job performance, particularly positive feedback. In general, praise will be infrequent; even when given, it is likely to be given awkwardly. It should be remembered that giving direct feedback to subordinates, particularly positive feedback, is a skill most Japanese managers do not possess.

An American manager also can help smooth relationships by disseminating information widely, and by avoiding any appearance of tooting her own horn. This flies in the face of most recommendations made in the popular press to American workers concerning the necessity of making sure your boss knows of your work successes. Japanese managers are trained to be very aware of the job performance of their subordinates. In addition, the involvement of the Japanese manager in the American manager's job—the "interference" mentioned above—means the Japanese manager is very aware of the day-to-day activities of the American manager.

A third technique that American managers can use is to see themselves as teaching their Japanese managers. Most Japanese managers are trained to be good listeners. When differences in management style become truly important and it is apparent that the difference is causing problems, it may be appropriate to discuss the difference with the Japanese manager. At the same time, it is important to avoid becoming angry during the discussion; anger is not perceived by the Japanese as reflecting the importance of an issue, but rather as showing lack of self-discipline. It may take several discussions of an issue before the Japanese manager understands the American manager's viewpoint; even then, the solution reached may be different from what is expected.

Finally, learning as much about Japanese culture as possible is helpful. It always helps to know what irksome behavior on the part of another person is actually the *norm* for his society—it helps to depersonalize the discomfort. There are a number of books on the subject of Japanese business and business practices, but two that might provide good starting points are Zimmerman's *How to Do Business with the Japanese* (1985) and Abegglen and Stalk's *Kaisha* (1985).

Learning to work successfully with a Japanese boss obviously entails broadening the cross-cultural skills of American managers. Acquiring these skills can be a great benefit in a era in which the American work force itself is becoming increasingly culturally diverse. Thus, even if the American manager chooses to leave the Japanese firm after a few years, the attempt to learn new behaviors and attitudes will be of value in working in a U.S.-owned firm. However, as can be seen from the discussion of issues in this article, achieving a good working relationship with a Japanese boss is a challenge—and not everyone may want to accept this challenge. Perhaps the most important point is that any American manager considering working for a Japanese firm should realistically asses her ability and desire to undertake the challenges outlined above.

Changes: Japanese Managers. For Japanese managers working in the U.S., several suggestions can be drawn from this discussion. Probably the most useful approach Japanese managers can take in learning how to manage American managers is to learn as much as possible about American management itself—its underlying assumptions and recommended techniques. Through understanding American approaches to management, it becomes easier to comprehend what American managers expect from a boss. Almost all management training in the U.S., for example, stresses the importance of clarity of communication between boss and subordinate, particularly regarding job expectations and feedback. This contrasts sharply with the dictate most Japanese subordinates learn of "hear one, understand ten"—meaning it is the subordinate's duty to interpret his boss' desires from minimal communication. A Japanese manager can learn more about American management through activities such as reading American self-help books aimed at American managers, e.g., the popular *One Minute Manager* (Blanchard and Johnson, 1982) or by asking American managers in his firm what books on management they have particularly enjoyed. He also should read texts used to teach university courses in the U.S. on management and organization behavior or, better yet, take a course at a local university or community college.

Understanding is an important first step. Equally important, however, is the need to acquire the skills of American management—particularly in areas such as conducting performance appraisals, giving daily feedback, and requesting a subordinate to do something. Japanese managers usually lack these necessary skills for managing American employees. In addition, Japanese managers need to learn how to "let go" of control—how to avoid interfering in the jobs of the American managers they hire and how to recognize what is considered as "interference." They also need to learn how to include American managers in important strategic decisions, and how to avoid behavior that is considered insensitive to Americans (such as speaking Japanese in front of them). In *The Japan that Can Say No*, Morita and Ishihara (1989) chastise their countrymen for behavior that segregates them from Americans; they encourage adopting attitudes and behavior of neighbors and co-workers while in the U.S.

Acquiring these new skills and attitudes is a challenging process that can be greatly aided by appropriate cross-cultural training. Research has shown that cross-cultural training can increase the success of overseas managers (Black and Mendenhall, 1990). Many reputable consulting and training firms in both the U.S. and Japan can provide help in this area. The investment in broadening a Japanese manager's skills may be costly, but it can produce benefits beyond increasing his effectiveness in managing U.S. managers. Given the changing values and attitudes of young Japanese workers—and the pressure for change this is putting on management systems in Japan—the Japanese manager who returns to Japan with these new skills will be better prepared to deal with the new demands on him.

One word of caution: of course, the role of the Japanese manager while in the U.S. is relevant to what skills he will need to be successful (Tung, 1981). Obviously, a short-term technical troubleshooter probably would have less need for the kinds of skills and training suggested above.

Conclusion

The challenges facing American and Japanese managers working in Japanese subsidiaries are considerable due to large differences in management style and lack of experience for both parties in working in this new environment. Like the trade imbalance between the two countries, the conflicts likely will continue and perhaps even increase before understanding leads to changes in behavior on both sides. However, it is important to see this as an opportunity for both sides to change in ways that could ultimately be of great benefit to management in their own countries.

References

Abegglen, J.C. and Stalk, G. Jr. *Kaisha*. New York: Basic Books, 1985.

Black, J.S. and Mendenhall, M. "Cross-Cultural Training Effectiveness: A Review and Theoretical Framework for Future Research," *The Academy of Management Review*, 1990, 15, pp. 113–136.

Blanchard, K. and Johnson, S. *One Minute Manager*. New York: Morrow, 1982.

Morita, A. *Made in Japan*. Reading, U.K.: Fontana/Collins, 1987.

Morita, A. and Ishihara, S. *The Japan that Can Say "No"*. Unofficial translation of book published in Japanese, 1989.

Pucik, V., Hanada, M., and Fifield, G. "Management Culture and Effectiveness of Local Executives in Japanese-owned U.S. Corporations." Working paper, University of Michigan Graduate School of Business, Ann Arbor, MI, July 1989.

Sullivan, J.J., Albrecht, T., and Taylor, S. "Process, Organizational, Relational, and Personal Determinants of Managerial Compliance-Gaining with Key Subordinates," *Journal of Business Communications*, in press.

Sullivan, J.J. and Taylor, S. "A Cross-cultural Test of Compliance-gaining Theory," National Academy of Management Meetings, Washington, D.C., 1989.

Tung, R. "Selection and Training of Personnel for Overseas Assignments," *Columbia Journal of World Business*, 1981, 16, pp. 68–78.

Zimmerman, M. *How to do Business with the Japanese*. Tokyo: Charles E. Tuttle, 1985.

EXERCISE: JAPANESE SERVICES/AMERICAN CONSUMERS

Introduction. This set of exercises gives you an opportunity to look at some of the cultural differences between Japan and the United States that may affect consumer expectations and behavior. Although the Japanese excel in producing high-quality manufactured goods, they are not as well-known as Americans for their ability to operate service industries, such as luxury hotels and resorts. In each of the scenarios described below, you will be asked to determine how different cultural assumptions may need to be modified in order to conform to the expectations of consumers in selected markets.

Scenario I:

JAPANESE HOTEL/RESTAURANT IN THE UNITED STATES

A Japanese hotel/restaurant conglomerate has decided to open a chain of hotels in various American resorts. These hotels will be comparable to three- and four-star American hotels like Radisson, Four Seasons, and Hyatt Regency. While the parent company will be Japanese, the staff at these hotels will be predominantly American, and the target market is Americans as well.

Your group has been hired as American consultants to advise the Japanese owners about what American consumers expect in a hotel and restaurant complex such as the one described here. Begin your work by appointing a spokesperson for the group who will report your findings to the larger group. Then, using the cultural assumptions outlined below, plus knowledge you have about Japan, develop a list of recommendations for the Japanese company that addresses these issues:

1. What do the Japanese owners need to know about the expectations of American *consumers* in order to design and manage a resort hotel and restaurant complex in the United States?

2. What do the Japanese owners need to know about the expectations of American *employees* who will staff these complexes?

As you discuss your answers to these questions, consider these aspects of the hotel and restaurant: rooms (size, type of furnishings, and so on), activities available at the complex, room service, service in the dining rooms, and type of food offered to guests. Consider also whether there should be a Japanese flavor to the hotel, or whether the Japanese ownership should be completely disguised.

CULTURAL ASSUMPTIONS

Listed below are some general cultural assumptions about individuals in the United States and in Japan. Because these are just generalizations, we cannot assume that they apply to all Americans or to all Japanese. However, they do describe typical characteristics of many Americans and of many Japanese and are therefore useful in planning business ventures for consumers in these two countries.

American	Japanese
Impatient	Patient
Informal in relationships	Formal in relationships
Action oriented	Affiliation oriented
Individualistic	Socialistic
Concerned with success	Concerned with losing face
Need a lot of private space	Need little private space

Scenario II:

JAPANESE CRUISE SHIP, AMERICAN PASSENGERS

A Japanese hotel company has formed a partnership with a Japanese shipbuilding company to start a luxury cruise line. The primary market for the cruise ships will be Americans, but the crew and staff will be Japanese.

Your group has been hired as American consultants to advise the Japanese owners about what American consumers expect from luxury cruise ships such as the ones described here. Begin your work by appointing a spokesperson for the group who will report your findings to the larger group. Then, using the cultural assumptions outlined below, plus knowledge you have about Japan, develop a list of recommendations for the Japanese company that addresses these issues:

1. What do the Japanese owners need to know about the expectations of *American consumers* in order to design and manage a luxury cruise ship line that will appeal to Americans?

2. What kind of training do the Japanese owners need to give the *Japanese employees* who will staff these ships?

As you discuss your answers to these questions, consider these aspects of the cruise ships: rooms (size, type of furnishings, and so on), activities available on board ship, room service, service in the dining rooms, type of food offered to guests, pricing, and tipping practices.[1]

CULTURAL ASSUMPTIONS

Listed below are some general cultural assumptions about individuals in the United States and in Japan. Because these are just generalizations, we cannot assume that they apply to all Americans or to all Japanese. However, they do describe typical characteristics of many Americans and of many Japanese and are therefore useful in planning business ventures for consumers in these two countries.

American	Japanese
Impatient	Patient
Informal in relationships	Formal in relationships
Action oriented	Affiliation oriented
Individualistic	Socialistic
Concerned with success	Concerned with losing face
Need a lot of private space	Need little private space

---

[1] In the late 1970s, the Soviet government attempted to enter the luxury cruise line business as one means of increasing its supply of hard currency. The *Odessa* was one of their ships that sailed the Caribbean routes. At that time, the Soviet concept of luxury and good food did not match the expectations of American cruise customers, and negative word-of-mouth reports hurt the Soviet efforts to penetrate the American market. The concept of consumer behavior research was an unknown concept for the Soviets at that time.

EXERCISE: NEGOTIATING WITH THE JAPANESE

In this exercise, you will have the opportunity to participate in planning and executing a negotiation session between the representatives of an American manufacturing firm and a Japanese venture capital company. Your instructor will assign individual roles during your class session. Some of you will represent the Japanese team and some will represent the American team. The rest of the class will make up an Observer Team and will offer a critique of how well the Japanese and American teams performed their negotiating roles.

Before you begin your planning sessions, read the article in this section entitled "Negotiating with the Americans." This article was written by a Japanese business person; it will give you some insights about how the Japanese conduct their business negotiations and how they view American negotiating styles. Pick out the differences between the two and use these as a planning tool in developing the strategies for the Japanese and American teams.

NEGOTIATING WITH THE AMERICANS

As far as it is known, this article is an unpublished essay written by a Japanese negotiator. The English translation was obtained in Tokyo by a U.S. contractor and provides some interesting perspectives on how the Japanese view American negotiating practices.

James T. Felicita, contributor of the article, is a former U.S. government contract negotiator and currently head of contracts for NASA Systems Div., Hughes Aircraft Co. He is a member of the Los Angeles/South Bay Chapter of NCMA.

At the start I must apologize for stating my ideas on this subject so boldly when my superiors already know more than I about the subject. I have had more than five years experience in dealing with U.S. negotiators and in all modesty report my findings in the hope that others can benefit. The subject deserves high evaluation and many hours of intense study so that we understand better our American friends.

Reprinted from *Contract Management* with permission of the publisher.

Background

U.S. negotiators are difficult to understand because they come from a background of different nationalities and experiences. Unlike Japanese the Americans are not racially or culturally homogeneous. Even their way of speaking English varies. Gaining a good understanding of one U.S. representative is only a little help in understanding others. Americans from large cities are different from those coming from small towns. There are differences between east and west, north and south, as well as in religion and national origin. Thus much of what they do is truly unpredictable and erratic. At the same time there is reason to suspect that beneath *the rather disorderly appearance of U.S. negotiating teams whose members often seem not to be listening to each other* and who may not even dress in the same style, there is a calculated set of tactics and objectives which guides them. Sometimes U.S. representatives seem to make mistakes or to be ignorant of commonly known facts, but their lack of humility in such cases may mean that they really know what they are doing.

The background of American history is an important influence on their attitudes. The American frontier was a major factor from the arrival of the first settlers from Europe and for about 250 years. American books describe how the west was conquered or won. In some strange way the empty spaces of America had to be captured from nature which was like an enemy. This is a complete contrast to our idea that one must live in harmony with nature.

Americans also highly value what they call adversary proceedings. This seems to come from their court system where two sides argue their cases in a direct confrontation with no effort made to find any harmony at all. Then the judge issues a ruling one way or the other without private consultations with the two sides and with no value given to conciliating the feelings of those in the case. Americans believe this undemocratic system is the best way to learn the truth and impose justice.

Americans sometimes say "truth is relative," or the "there is no such thing as black and white, only shades of grey," but often they act differently. They are seekers of truth and morality, just as we are, but they think truth and morality exist apart from the practical world around them. So in a negotiation it is common for American negotiators to say what basic principles are important. Later they may reject a sound practical idea because it violates principle. Therefore it is necessary to be cautious about agreeing to any statement of principles and always point out the need for workable understandings. One possibility is that their fixed ideas about truth come from Christian religion which promises perfection at some future time or after death, so many American negotiators try to negotiate perfect and final agreements which they think will never need reinterpretation or adjustment. Indeed, once an agreement is signed they may be very rigid about it because they think it is perfect. As to Christianity, I am not sure what it teaches because there are many different kinds of Christians.

Americans have had a world leadership role since the end of World War II. They understand and are proud of their status, but seem not to know how they got there. They often talk about how hard we Japanese work, but many Americans work hard and they can be extremely clever sometimes. However, they seem to attribute their leadership status not to hard work but to the idea that they know the truth and are moral. Thus they are convinced that their ideas are right and others must follow or reveal themselves as fools or knaves. This may seem a harsh

judgement, and it is overstated, but Americans are often ethnocentric without knowing it. Americans also take as given the tremendous wealth of their country, including rich deposits of minerals and petroleum as well as agricultural land. They waste these resources as if there were no end to them, spreading out over the land inefficiently and seeming not to notice.

U.S. Negotiating Preparations

Without access to their secrets I can only guess, from their behavior and what they tell me, how the Americans prepare for negotiations. They have procedures much like ours, but sometimes seem not to follow them. Often *they argue among themselves in public, so it is safe to assume they argue even more in private*. This is part of their idea of adversary proceedings, and they seem to feel no shame about such embarrassing behavior.

The procedures they use include careful study of the Japanese position, the reasons for it, and the negotiating pressure each side can apply. They spend the most time on their own position. Like the Japanese government they have many different agencies with different interests which must be reconciled. This is done by circulating draft papers and holding meetings at which middle level officials discuss what to do. Each of these officials represents his own superiors and has limited power to express his own ideas, unlike Japanese officials at that level whose advice is usually accepted since they have more time to study and become experts on detailed matters.

U.S. negotiators often have fallback positions which they can use if they do not win agreement to first proposals. These fallbacks are worked out in advance almost as if they knew their first offers were unreasonable. They do not prepare one approach as the best under the circumstances, while giving their negotiators authority to approach the matter flexibly. Therefore it is necessary for us to learn what the final fallback is as early as possible. Once that information is obtained it is often possible to get the U.S. side to offer its fallback proposal in return for a concession of no consequence.

The Americans also try to predict what our reactions will be. They prepare contingency plans which they hope will counter our statements, again believing that confrontation and rebuttal are necessary.

They seem to value highly winning such arguments. When arguments do develop U.S. negotiators may become tense, after which they may try to distract attention from a difficult situation by resorting to humor. Their humor is hard to understand since it is based on their own rather strange cultural experience, but it is safe to laugh when they do.

In the Negotiating Room

U.S. negotiating teams are sometimes small and sometimes large. Their delegations are often large when the internal disagreements between agencies have not been reconciled before the meeting, and therefore each department (or sub-department) must send an agent. On the other hand, they often limit the number on their side, perhaps because of internal jealousy. They do not always admit observers from interested agencies and seldom have anyone present for training purposes or as an extra notetaker. Thus our delegation is usually larger. Americans are not used to having cameramen in the meeting room and may be surprised when they encounter a large group of photographers when they arrive. Secretly, however, they seem to like the show as if it were a kind of flattery and not just the curiosity of our press representatives who compete so hard with each other.

Americans are quite conscious of protocol, so it is necessary to consider seating and the matter of introductions and entertainment. They often say that rank means nothing to them, but it really does. On the other hand when mistakes are made they adapt easily and are not offended if the matter is quietly corrected. In short, they want the proper gestures made but are satisfied with that. They also like to be invited to social events where they say they dislike discussing business and then in fact they easily agree to do so. Such occasions are useful for testing compromises and obtaining information on their fallback positions.

The Progress of Talks

Americans are energetic and persistent. They are enthusiastic negotiators who seldom take naps during talks even if the topic at hand is of no real concern. They enjoy arguing the logic of their position which they like to describe as good for all and not just for them. They have a disturbing habit, however, of passing over very quickly the areas of agreement and giving high emphasis to disagreements. In fact they talk about little else, as if that were the most important subject!

Americans like to concentrate on one problem at a time. They seem not to understand that the whole picture is more important, and they spend little time on developing a general understanding of the views and interests of both sides. Since their habit of focusing on one issue often forces a direct disagreement they often propose setting the issue aside, but then they come back to it later with the same attitude and concentration. A negotiation with them may therefore become a series of small conflicts, and we must always make a special effort to give proper attention to the large areas of agreement and common interests.

During negotiations the Americans sometimes forget that we are frequently called upon to brief the press and that events in the talks may be fully described in our newspapers. It is necessary to explain to them that this is our idea of how a free press works and that un-attributed reports on the progress of negotiations are useful to prepare the public for the final results. It is helpful to discuss with them in advance the subjects which can be described to the press. Usually they will then agree to general briefing, but if this is not done they may complain about the reports they did not expect to see in the newspapers. When our press people force us to say more than we had agreed we would say, the Americans profess to be quite disturbed.

When talks are concluded the U.S. side always feels some kind of euphoria, they like to think they have won, which is part of the adversary style common to them. They may engage in some public gloating to justify themselves to their countrymen. This is annoying when they do, but I suppose we should try to understand such behavior and recognize that they really cannot help themselves and do not mean any harm.

CASE STUDY: MANAGING A MULTIETHNIC WORK FORCE IN FRANCE

Until the end of the Second World War, France had an extensive colonial empire. Its empire included colonies in Africa, Southeast Asia, and the West Indies. Unlike the British, who usually regarded native populations in their colonies as non-British, the French considered the native populations in their colonies to be part of *"la grande France,"* that is, French citizens in the same way that French natives in Europe were French citizens. As a result of this attitude, it was fairly easy for natives of French colonies to emigrate to European France both before and after French rule ended.

French employers brought many colonial workers to France to provide labor for construction, mining, the car industry, and seasonal agriculture. These workers then brought their families to France as soon as they could afford to do so, and today, France's population includes many immigrants from Vietnam, Algeria, Morocco, and the West Indies.

Your company has decided to expand its operations to France. You have just acquired a manufacturing facility that makes parts for the French automobile industry. The plant is already fully staffed and most of the workers perform assembly line functions. Rather than hiring new workers and training them, you have determined that it is most cost-effective to retain the current employees. But you also know that there have been some problems in this plant because the French managers were not very adept at handling cultural and ethnic differences.

The employees at your newly acquired plant include first- and second-generation immigrants from Vietnam, Algeria, and Morocco, as well as French natives. These individuals come from different religious backgrounds, including Roman Catholicism, Confucianism, Buddhism, and Islam; they speak different native languages, although all of them speak at least some French; and their historical perspectives are different, that is, the immigrants come from families who were natives of areas colonized by the French, while the French natives come from families who were the colonizers.

Instructions: Discuss your answers to the following questions:

1. What are some of the general cultural and historical differences among these workers that will make it difficult to run a harmonious plant?

2. How would you counsel American managers about coping with and mediating these differences?

3. What are the similarities between this situation and that found in American plants that employ workers from diverse cultural and ethnic groups? What are the differences?

SUGGESTED READINGS

Ardagh, John. *France Today.* London: Penguin Books, 1990.

Braudel, Fernand. *The Identity of France, Vol. 2: People and Production.* Translated by Siân Reynolds. New York: HarperCollins, 1990. (See especially pp. 203–220)

"Jam for the Beurs, France's North African Arab Immigrants." *The Economist* 306, no. 7540 (March 5, 1988): 52.

Lawday, David. "Scorned Today, Hailed Tomorrow? Europe's Post-1992 Economy Will Badly Need Immigrant Skills and Muscle." *Newsweek,* January 30, 1989: 51–54.

"Tradition Plays an Important Role in French Business." *Business America* 112, no. 9 (May 6, 1991): 22–23.

Wilson, Frank L. "Business and Workplace Democratization in France." *Business in the Contemporary World* 3, no. 4 (Summer 1991): 55–58.

CASE STUDY: FISH FARMING ENTERPRISE IN MEXICO

Amica Corporation is a specialty construction equipment company based in Albuquerque, New Mexico. Established five years ago by a chemical engineer, Arthur Jackson, the company's business plan is to sell the firm within the next 12–18 months and invest the capital in another venture. Jackson has identified a channel catfish farm as his next project. His family owned a small fish farm in Louisiana, so he has most of the technical knowledge needed for that kind of business. In addition, this project fits his goal of combining business profits with socially responsible actions.

The catfish farm operation Jackson is planning will be a self-contained, full-cycle production plant. It will include a hatchery, fishery ponds, and a processing plant. He expects to realize economy of scale by combining all these functions in one location. Ordinarily, the farming portion of the operation is separate from the processing plant, thus requiring transportation to the plant in addition to transportation to the end consumer.

After careful analysis of the financial factors, Jackson has decided to locate the fish farm and plant in a small town in Mexico. This decision is based on several considerations:

1. Both land and labor are cheaper in Mexico than in the United States.

2. A plentiful, cheap water supply, essential to a fish farming operation, is available in Mexico.

3. The warmer climate in the Mexican lowlands means a shorter maturation time for the fish than is true in the Mississippi delta region, the center of U.S. catfish farming operations.

4. According to a Mexican trade magazine and government representatives, Mexico is interested in importing agricultural products from the United States. These same sources note an increase in fish consumption per capita in Mexico for the same reasons as the similar increase in the United States—lower cholesterol and lower cost than other protein sources.

Although the laws regarding a foreign company owning a business in Mexico have been relaxed, for example, businesses valued under $100 million do not require a Mexican partner, Jackson has determined that political, social, and cultural factors, as well as business and financial considerations, argue for a Mexican partner. His Mexican partner will be familiar with Mexican laws, with how to get through the Mexican bureaucratic system when setting up a business, and with Mexican morés related to work.

Amica Corporation expects to hire some U.S. personnel to staff the Mexican operation, including an ichthyologist, an aquaculturist, and a production manager for the packing plant. The company will hire all other personnel in Mexico.

While profit is the primary goal, Jackson and his associates hope to realize a secondary goal of providing inexpensive, high-quality protein to their customers in Mexico and the United States. As rivers, lakes, and oceans become increasingly polluted, and as consumption of fish increases, this source of protein becomes increasingly more expensive. By producing fish in a controlled environment without pollutants and close to the consumer, Jackson expects to capitalize on an unfilled market niche and provide part of the local population's nutritional needs. In addition to looking at what advantages Mexico offers his company, Jackson is also considering what advantages his company's being there affords the local population.

Recognizing that U.S.-Mexican relations have often been characterized by war, territorial disputes, and misunderstandings, and that there are significant differences between U.S. and Mexican cultures, Jackson has hired your group to do a cultural analysis for him. While his Mexican partner will be able to answer many of these questions and will do much to ease relations between U.S. and Mexican personnel, Jackson believes a U.S. group's analysis will complement the Mexican perspective.

Your group's first move was to consult the Consul-General of Mexico at his office in Denver. During your two-hour meeting with the Consul-General, you discussed several of the subtle differences between Mexican and U.S. cultures and how a knowledge of these differences is important to business success in Mexico.

Instructions: What will you tell Arthur Jackson at Amica Corporation about the following cultural characteristics as they relate to his proposed business venture in Mexico?

1. Language
2. Management practices
3. Values related to work
4. Time
5. Religion
6. Social class structure
7. Gender roles
8. Family relationships

SUGGESTED READINGS

Becker, Thomas. "Where to Invest in Mexico." *Management Review* 80, no. 6 (June 1991): 22–25.

———. "Taboos and How To's about Earning an Honest Peso." *Management Review* 80, no. 6 (June 1991): 16–21.

Condon, John. *Good Neighbors: Communicating with the Mexicans*. Yarmouth, Maine: Intercultural Press, 1985.

Guillermoprieto, Alma. "Report from Mexico: Serenading the Future." *New Yorker* 68, no. 38 (November 9, 1992): 96–104.

Jarvis, Susan. "Preparing Employees to Work South of the Border." *Personnel* 67, no. 6 (June 1990): 59–63.

"Mexico: A New Era." *Business Week*, November 12, 1990: 102.

Paz, Octavio. *The Labyrinth of Solitude: Life and Thought in Mexico*. Translated by Lysander Kemp. New York: Grove Press, 1961.

Riding, Alan. *Distant Neighbors: A Portrait of the Mexicans*. New York: Knopf, 1985.

CASE STUDY: TIME/SPACE/NONVERBAL COMMUNICATION: AMERICAN AND PUERTO RICAN MANAGERS

Introduction

"Time is money."

"Don't stand so close. You're breathing down my neck."

There are many different ideas about the values of time and space among peoples of the world. The feelings expressed in the comments above are typical of the ideas held by many Americans about the value of time and about the appropriate amount of physical space an individual should leave between one person and another.

Let's take a look first at the idea of time. Benjamin Franklin was probably the first American to point out that wasting time is like wasting money; Franklin asked (and answered), "Dost thou love life? Then do not squander time, for that is the stuff life is made of." And many, if not most, Americans agree with the wisdom of that idea. For example, imagine yourself seated in a restaurant, waiting for a friend who is scheduled to meet you at noon for lunch. You look at your watch and see that it's already 12:20. You begin to wonder where your friend could be. You're probably a little concerned that your friend might have had an accident, but you're probably also a little annoyed at being kept waiting. Finally,

about 12:45, your friend comes in, says hello, sits down, and then asks, "Well, what do you think we should have for lunch today?" If you're like most Americans, you are probably astonished that your friend did not explain being 45 minutes late. But if you were in a country in South America, for example, you might not consider your friend's behavior at all unusual or impolite.

Now let's consider another aspect of cultural values—physical space. When Americans are introduced to a new person, for example, a business associate, most Americans lean forward slightly, shake hands with the new man or woman, then take a step or two backwards to put a comfortable amount of space between themselves and the person they have just met. Think about how you would feel in this same situation, if the person you have just been introduced to were to step *forward* after shaking hands, thereby reducing the space between the two of you to about four or five inches. You might feel uncomfortable standing this close to a stranger; in fact, you might begin to back away, thinking, "Don't stand so close. You're breathing down my neck." Conversely, the person from the other culture may be wondering why you are stepping away. Having always heard that Americans were outgoing and friendly, your stepping back indicates that you are very unfriendly.

All cultures have specific values related to time and space. When your culture's values relating to time or space conflict with another culture's values, as in the case of the business associate who stood too close for "cultural" comfort, misunderstandings or even animosity may occur between people from the different cultures. This can be uncomfortable if you're traveling in another country; it can be even more serious, however, if you are doing business in the other country.

Edward Hall identified two types of time: monochronic and polychronic. In cultures where monochronic time is the dominant mode, as in most parts of the United States, individuals tend to concentrate on one activity or one project at a time. When they are at the office, work takes precedence over personal concerns. In cultures where polychronic time characterizes the way most people organize their time, there is not as clear a delineation between different types of activities. Individuals in these cultures are more apt to be involved in several things at a time. For a business person from a monochronic time culture, it can be disconcerting to have an important business meeting interrupted while the host from the polychronic time culture takes telephone calls from a spouse or, as in the case of the luncheon engagement, to be kept waiting for 45 minutes with no explanation. The monochronic time person often views this behavior as impolite, inconsiderate, or bad business, while the polychronic time person is acting in a normal way according to other cultural norms.

As we increase our business and social contacts with people from other parts of the world, we also need to increase our understanding of their cultural values. Behaviors and gestures that are perfectly acceptable in one cultural context can take on new and different meanings in another cultural context. To avoid such cultural misunderstandings, we must be aware first of our own culturally determined behavior in order to understand the culturally determined behavior of others. These concepts are treated in more detail in the books by anthropologist Edward Hall entitled *The Silent Language* and *The Hidden Dimension*.

In the following scene between two business associates, Juan Perillo and Jean Moore, you will see the consequences of such a clash in cultural values.

SUGGESTED READINGS

Hall, Edward T. *The Hidden Dimension.* New York: Doubleday, 1966.

———. *The Silent Language.* New York: Doubleday, 1981.

———. "The Silent Language of Overseas Business." *Harvard Business Review* 38, no. 3 (1960): 87–96.

EXERCISE: SCRIPT FOR JUAN PERILLO AND JEAN MOORE

SCENE I: February 15, San Juan, Puerto Rico

Juan: Welcome back to Puerto Rico, Jean. It is good to have you here in San Juan again. I hope that your trip from Dayton was a smooth one.

Jean: Thank you, Juan. It's nice to be back here where the sun shines. Fred sends his regards and also asked me to tell you how important it is that we work out a firm production schedule for the next three months. But first, how is your family? All doing well, I hope.

Juan: My wife is doing very well, but my daughter, Marianna, broke her arm and has to have surgery to repair the bone. We are very worried about that because the surgeon says she may have to have several operations. It is very difficult to think about my poor little daughter in the operating room. She was out playing with some other children when it happened. You know how rough children sometimes play with each other. It's really amazing that they don't have more injuries. Why, just last week, my son. . . .

Jean: Of course I'm very sorry to hear about little Marianna, but I'm sure everything will go well with the surgery. Now, shall we start work on the production schedule?

Juan: Oh, yes, of course, we must get started on the production schedule.

Jean: Fred and I thought that June 1 would be a good cutoff date for the first phase of the schedule. And we also thought that 100 A-type computers would be a reasonable goal for that phase. We know that you have some new assemblers whom you are training, and that you've had some problems getting parts from your suppliers in the past few months. But we're sure you have all of those problems worked out by now and that you are back to full production capability. So, what do you think? Is 100 A-type computers produced by June 1 a reasonable goal for your people?

Juan: (Hesitates a few seconds before replying) You want us to produce 100 of the newly designed A-type computers by June 1? Will we also be producing our usual number of Z-type computers, too?

Jean: Oh, yes. Your regular production schedule would remain the same as it's always been. The only difference is that you would be producing the new A-type computers, too. I mean, after all, you have a lot of new employees, and you have all of the new manufacturing and assembling equipment that we have in Dayton. So, you're as ready to make the new product as we are.

Juan: Yes, that's true. We have the new equipment and we've just hired a lot of new assemblers who will be working on the A-type computer. I guess there's no reason we can't meet the production schedule you and Fred have come up with.

Jean: Great, great. I'll tell Fred you agree with our decision and will meet the goal of 100 A-type computers by June 1. He'll be delighted to know that you can deliver what he was hoping for. And, of course, Juan, that means that you'll be doing just as well as the Dayton plant.

Scene II: May 1, San Juan, Puerto Rico

Jean: Hello, Juan. How are things here in Puerto Rico? I'm glad to have the chance to come back and see how things are going.

Juan: Welcome, Jean. It's good to have you here. How is your family?

Jean: Oh, they're fine, just fine. You know, Juan, Fred is really excited about that big order we just got from the Defense Department for 50 A-type computers. They want them by June 10, so we will ship them directly to Washington from San Juan as the computers come off your assembly line. Looks like it's a good thing we set your production goal at 100 A-type computers by June 1, isn't it?

Juan: Um, yes, that was certainly a good idea.

Jean: So, tell me. Have you had any problems with the new model? How are your new assemblers working out? Do you have any suggestions for changes in the manufacturing specs? How is the new quality control program working with this model? We're always looking for ways to improve, you know, and we appreciate any ideas you can give us.

Juan: Well, Jean, there is one thing. . . .

Jean: Yes? What is that?

Juan: Well, Jean, we have had a few problems with the new assemblers. Three of them have had serious illnesses in their families and have had to take off several days at a time to nurse a sick child or elderly parent. And another one was involved in a car accident and was in the hospital for several days. And you remember my daughter's surgery? Well, her arm didn't mend properly and we had to take her to Houston for additional consultations and therapy. But, of course, you and Fred knew about that.

Jean: Yes, we were aware that you had had some personnel problems and that you and your wife had had to go to Houston with Marianna. But what does that have to do with the 50 A-type computers for the Defense Department?

Juan: Well, Jean, because of all these problems, we have had a few delays in the production schedule. Nothing serious, but we are a little bit behind our schedule.

Jean: How far behind is "a little bit"? What are you trying to tell me, Juan? Will you have 50 more A-type computers by June 1 to ship to Washington to fill the Defense Department order?

Juan: Well, I certainly hope we will have that number ready to ship. You know how difficult it can be to predict a precise number for manufacturing, Jean. You probably have many of these same problems in the Dayton plant, don't you?

CASE STUDY: AN AMERICAN MANUFACTURER AND THE EUROPEAN COMMUNITY

Bill Radetsky eased his rental car onto the Autobahn at the outskirts of Stuttgart and headed southeast toward Munich. Glancing at the dashboard clock, he realized that it was only 10:00 a.m., six hours before his flight to Chicago was to leave Flughafen Riem, Munich's international airport. Since Stuttgart and Munich are only 200 kilometres (120 miles) apart, Bill decided to find a scenic town for lunch somewhere between the two cities. He pulled off the Autobahn at the next rest stop and looked at his travel guide. Ulm appeared to be midway between the two cities and boasts the world's highest cathedral spire, according to the Michelin guide.

"That sounds good," thought Bill. "I'll stop there and find a Gasthaus for lunch and have a look around the city center."

In Ulm, Bill found a small café in the middle of town and took a seat by the window where he could watch people milling about on the Platz. The cathedral, with its 161.5-meter spire, was directly across the way and dominated the entire city.

As he settled in the comfortable chair, Bill thought back over the events of the last ten days. He had accomplished everything he had planned for this trip, and even had had some time for a brief sightseeing excursion in Augsburg. Now he was looking forward to getting back to the office in the United States and reporting to the managers at Grand Lakes Manufacturing (GLM) about the accomplishments of this trip.

Bill was GLM's national sales manager. He had worked for Grand Lakes Manufacturing for more than twenty years and had been a strong advocate of the company's expan-

sion to Europe. Planning for that expansion had started more than two years ago and Bill was returning from this trip with a large order from a German automobile parts firm.

GLM is a 30-year-old firm located on the outskirts of Chicago; its annual sales total $32 million and it has 175 employees. The company manufactures transfer presses[2] for the automotive and appliance industries, and provides engineering design services to various large manufacturers in several midwestern states.

The company decided to explore sales potential in Europe for several reasons. About five years ago, the company began receiving requests for information from companies in Europe and Asia. At the same time, several of GLM's U.S. customers who had ties with European companies recommended GLM to the European partners. After selling two large presses to European companies, GLM decided to pursue that market more vigorously.

The company's founder and president, John Rein, assigned primary planning responsibility for the European venture to one of the company's vice-presidents, Joanne Richards. John believed that his company, and any other U.S. company for that matter, had a great deal to learn by looking at competitors in other parts of the world and talking to potential customers in those areas, even if they subsequently decided against exporting.

As part of her initial research on exporting to Europe, Joanne contacted the state's Economic Development Office and the U.S. Chamber of Commerce for information. The Economic Development Office's representative in Brussels provided general information about doing business in Europe, and he gave GLM the name of a German consultant, Klaus Barr, who works with American companies to establish contacts in Germany. The Chamber of Commerce also furnished the names of two American consultants who provide similar assistance. Joanne and several GLM managers interviewed the three consultants and asked for their proposals on what they would do if hired by GLM.

The American consultants proposed writing a business plan for GLM's European venture, plus setting up appointments with prospective German customers. Their fee was $25,000 and a commission on all sales made by the company during a specified time period. Herr Barr's proposal included securing appointments with German companies and accompanying GLM managers to these meetings, acting as an interpreter when necessary. His fee was $5,000 for preparing dossiers on the German companies and making the contacts; he charged $1,000 per day for the time spent with GLM managers in Germany. After considering both proposals, GLM chose Herr Barr's, because he was a German citizen and because he had executive contacts in the German tool and die and automotive industries through his family's business. Also, GLM wanted to purchase some specialized services, not acquire a business partner.

Bill mentally reviewed the events of that first trip to Germany as he drank a beer and waited for his lunch to be served. "Choosing Klaus as our consultant was probably the best decision we ever made," he thought. "His work directly contributed to the success we had on our first visit and to the success I've had on this second trip to Germany."

Klaus had secured appointments with the appropriate managers at several of Germany's largest automotive parts firms. In addition, he spent two days with GLM man-

---

[2] Transfer presses are a type of industrial equipment used in moving pieces of metal or other materials through several steps of the manufacturing process. GLM's presses would be used in the manufacture of automotive or appliance components.

agers, briefing them on what to do to prepare for the meetings and what to do during the meetings. As Klaus told them, "The cultural differences between Americans and Germans are still very important and must be considered when doing business in Germany. In particular, you need to be aware of German business protocol and of how the decision-making process works in German businesses."

The initial meetings between GLM and German managers were information meetings, not sales appointments. Klaus stressed the important distinction between these two types of meetings by explaining that before German managers want to know about a company's product, they want to know about the company itself. Is it a family owned company? What is its philosophy? Who are the company's key managers? What are they like to do business with?

Klaus suggested that GLM send several of its top managers on the first trip to Germany. Besides Bill Radetsky, two other top executives went on the trip—Dave Roberts, GLM's general manager, and Peter Streichen, the company's Canadian sales manager. Dave, in addition to being a senior level manager, is an engineer and has extensive technical knowledge about the company's products. Peter is also an engineer; moreover, he emigrated to Canada from Germany in the 1950s and speaks fluent German.

To complement Klaus's expertise about German business practices, Joanne hired a German-American woman to present a one-day seminar on German culture to several GLM managers. As Dave described it, "She covered the things you wouldn't think of, things that seemed at first like 'fluff,' but were actually critical information and showed that we had a real interest in and concern for German culture."

Among other things, the consultant advised them to wear a suit to all meetings with their German counterparts and not to remove the jacket as one might in a meeting with U.S. customers. Also, allow the German managers to suggest sharing a drink or a meal, rather than inviting them to be GLM's guests. Always address the German managers as "Herr ____" or "Frau____," she recommended, until they indicate that they want to be called by their first names.

Joanne and the GLM management team decided to translate the company's brochures into German and to make some modifications as a way of anticipating potential problems Klaus had pointed out to them. As Klaus explained, most German companies would be interested in GLM's products but might have some unspoken concerns or reservations. For example, if the company's brochure gave the product's dimensions in inches, a German customer would wonder if size would be a problem since Germans are accustomed to thinking in centimeters. Or, a customer might wonder, how do American safety and electrical standards compare to German standards? Do they conform to the Siemens standards adopted by European Community members? Finally, the German managers meeting with GLM's representatives would want to show the brochures to their employees, most of whom would not know English. And because the opinion of these employees is important in the decision to buy a product, it is important that they understand what that product can do.

After months of preparation, Bill and the other managers flew to Europe for the meetings Klaus had set up. Klaus met them at the Munich airport with detailed instructions on how to get from one location to the next and additional information about each company.

During the next six days, the GLM team followed Klaus's carefully designed plan and met with eight German companies in the Baden Württemburg region. Klaus accompanied the GLM managers to all meetings except one, and at each meeting, they carried out the strategy they had devised with Klaus's assistance.

The GLM managers arrived promptly for each meeting and were quickly ushered into a conference room where they met the German company's representatives. After some initial observations about the German company's facilities and its products, one of the GLM managers talked about GLM's history, its owners, its managers, and its operating philosophy. Then one of the U.S. managers asked several questions about the German company's general needs related to equipment, as well as questions about specific departments' needs. At some companies, the senior German manager insisted on conducting the meeting in English; in these instances, all three GLM managers participated in the discussion. At other companies, the discussion was in German and Peter presented the material about GLM and its products. While he talked to the German managers, Klaus simultaneously translated the exchange for Dave and Bill, who did not speak German.

In all but one or two of these meetings, the GLM managers were encouraged by their German hosts to stay longer than the time originally scheduled for the meeting. As the conversation moved beyond general information about GLM to specifics about the company's products, the German managers showed a great deal of interest and enthusiasm for knowing more details about GLM's transfer presses. As he thought back over these meetings, Bill recalled being nervous at the beginning of several of the meetings. But when the participants began to talk about GLM's products, he realized that the German managers were asking the same questions as American managers asked, and that the German managers appreciated the knowledge Bill and his colleagues offered. Three companies asked GLM to submit proposals for specific pieces of equipment.

In their debriefing with Klaus at the end of the trip, Bill and his colleagues decided on the following actions:

1. Write up individual notes and impressions of the trip and consolidate these in a single report to give all GLM managers. This detailed narrative of decision making and actions would become part of the "company memory," providing managers in the future a record of what to do if they decided to expand to other parts of the world. This was also a way of reminding all managers that their short-term actions often have long-term payoffs.

2. Modify the company's German language literature to correct some technical terms and to accommodate the changes suggested in some of the meetings. The GLM managers discovered that Peter's knowledge of German, while adequate for conversation, was 40 years old and had not kept up with the living language spoken in Germany today. After discovering some errors in the brochures, they decided to pay a German translation firm to do an initial translation and an American translator to do a back-translation.

3. Develop and send proposals to the three companies that requested them, and write thank you letters to the other companies. On the latter, Klaus recommended

that certain ones be written in German and the others in English, according to the language in which the meeting was conducted and who had set up the meeting.

4. Determine how to establish a service and parts center in Europe. In their discussions with the German companies, Bill and the others had assured their potential customers that GLM would have a continuing presence in Europe through a service center. As they had expected, German companies wanted to know that GLM planned to service, not just sell, its equipment in Europe. Moreover, the GLM managers recognized the need to staff this center with technically competent personnel who spoke German. As Klaus pointed out, the workers who would be using the equipment probably would not speak English; to avoid going through several levels of managers, GLM's service representatives need to speak German.

5. Schedule a second trip to Europe within the next three to four months to demonstrate GLM's commitment to and interest in potential European customers.

And now Bill was completing that second trip and returning to the United States with two large orders from German companies, as well as the prospect of several more orders in the next few months.

Instructions:

1. As this case study shows, GLM was very successful in its initial attempts to interest German companies in its products. What specific actions and decisions did GLM personnel take to ensure this success?

2. In addition to the five activities Bill and his colleagues outlined at the end of the trip, can you suggest other steps GLM managers need to implement as a follow-up to the first two trips?

3. What kind of organization would you recommend for GLM's European venture? Should they establish a permanent sales office in Europe? If so, how should they staff the office? Should they replicate their manufacturing plant in Europe? If they do establish a plant in Europe, who should head up the operation?

4. At the end of this question is some additional information about GLM and its organizational structure. After analyzing this structure, consider the recommendations you made in answering the previous question. What organizational changes, if any, do you think the corporation needs to make for each of the alternatives you identified?

Background Information and Organizational Structure for Grand Lakes Manufacturing

GLM is a family owned corporation, comprising three separate companies headed by the founder, John Rein. The organizational chart sketched on the next page outlines the man-

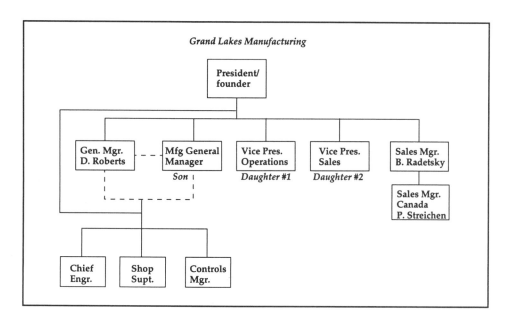

agement structure of the company that manufactures the transfer presses; it also shows the positions held by various family members in this company. Note the unusual configuration of reporting relationships connecting the general manager, the manufacturing general manager, and the plant personnel. These symbolize the triad type of relationship some managers describe themselves as having with the general manager, the manufacturing manager, and the president. The chief engineer, shop superintendent, and controls manager report to, and/or work closely with, all three of these people.

AMERICAN MANUFACTURING COMPETITIVENESS: THE VIEW FROM EUROPE

Robert S. Collins and William A. Fischer

If our products are so poor, why are we doing that well in Europe?

> *Richard Gephardt (D. Mo.)*
> *(quoted in Gordon 1992)*

Nineteen ninety-two is the 35th anniversary of *Business Horizons*, the 500th anniversary of the European discovery (or rediscovery) of the "New World," and the eve of the birth of the European Common Market. It is also an appropriate point to stop and reconsider the strength of the American industrial juggernaut vis-à-vis the continent with which, for much of its modern life, it has been irretrievably bound by inheritances of philosophical, political, and economic ties, as well as by the shared sacrifices of generations of citizens on both sides—in war and in emigration.

As the year began, America was looking considerably more eastward, toward the Orient, than it was across the Atlantic. Europe was felt to be considerably better known. As Representative Gephardt's sentiments reveal, for most Americans, Europe—that is, Western Europe—was most frequently thought of as a familiar, perhaps even somewhat tired, possibly even shopworn, collection of markets, which somehow or in some way would join together in the not-too-distant future to attempt to create a "United States of Europe," in obvious emulation of America's own success. The American business press, although increasingly paying more attention to the emerging Economic Community (especially when its behavior could be portrayed as "Fortress Europe") than was true of the general public, was also relatively sanguine about American industry's future there, no matter how the market worked out. After all, weren't

American firms already considerably more "pan-European" than their more nationalistic European rivals (Lipsey 1990)? And anyway, wasn't the whole idea of Fortress Europe to keep the Japanese, not the Americans, out? Even a casual reading of America's business press suggests a certain smugness regarding America's ability to "deal" with its European cousins.

Manufacturing was no exception to this arrogance. *The Machine That Changed the World* (Womack et al. 1990) showed clearly that even though American automakers were well behind the Japanese in creating lean manufacturing organizations, the Europeans were often even worse. In a world dazzled by Japan's ability to develop and commercialize an astonishing array of consumer products, European industrial science and technology was all but forgotten. The proliferation of McDonald's into the very hearts of Paris and Rome was seen as vivid testimony to the ultimate superiority of American operational skills in the service areas. American business schools crowded onto the pages of *The International Herald Tribune*, trumpeting their products as if Europeans should naturally be interested in buying them. In short, even a close reading of the American scene could not dispel the notion that for most Americans, Europe was not only well known, but, also in terms of industrial competitiveness, the challenge was in the Pacific Basin, not in the "Old World."

Global Competition: The European Perspective

Not surprisingly, most European managers do not see the future of industrial competition in quite the same way as do their American counterparts. In fact, because of these differences in perspective, European managers' views of American competitive resources are also quite different from those of Americans. We will present some of these perceptions in the hope that the view from outside may prove to be instructive for American businesses competing in the global marketplace.

Almost a decade ago, Kenichi Ohmae (1985) wrote of the growing convergence of world markets and the international proliferation of sophisticated technologies in what he called "the Triad." In his view, North America, Japan, and Western Europe had become the major actors in an unfolding global economy. This view has since remained useful for conceptualizing global commerce. Although it included Western Europe as one of three significant economic entities, it clearly focused on Japan and the U.S. as the principals.

A more provocative way to begin to examine European perceptions of U.S. manufacturing competitiveness, however, would be to start not with Ohmae and his triangular future, but with Jacques Attali, head of the newly formed European Bank for Reconstruction and Development, and long a close advisor to French President Francois Mitterrand. In his recently published *Millennium* (Attali 1991) he foresees a *bipolar* world, in which:

> . . . [i]n the next century, Japan and Europe may supplant the United States as the chief superpowers wrangling for global economic supremacy. Only a radical transformation of American society can forestall this development and its political consequences.

Furthermore.

> . . . if Western Europe is able to link Eastern Europe with its development, an integrated Europe has the chance to assume the role of the center of the world economy. It will then be able to develop as the most populated, the richest, and the most creative center in the world.

In Attali's new world order, it is the combination of new European strengths and American decline, particularly in manufacturing and technology, that lead inexorably to a distinctly subordinate role for the U.S., as part of the Japanese *hinterland*. Is he right? Is he sane? Can we really envision a world in which Europe and Japan, *and not the United States*, dominate the economic stage? Perhaps not, particularly since:

> When the final 1991 trade figures are added up, they will show that the U.S. ran a stunning $17 billion surplus with Europe, a nearly threefold increase over 1990's surplus of $6 billion. . . . Fueling the trade bonanza is a potent combination

of a cheap dollar, higher-quality products, and Yankee selling ingenuity. . . .The American trade juggernaut now has racked up its first surplus in 120 years with Germany, Europe's biggest economy, where American car imports have doubled in a year. Of the EC countries, only Italy continues to run a surplus with the U.S. (Melcher et al. 1992).

But the sentiment of Attali's statement, though exaggerated, is akin to much of what European managers said they felt about American manufacturing competitiveness. And right or wrong, it is their perceptions that will guide their behavior as competitors or collaborators in the global market.

European Perceptions Of Competitive Dimensions

Between the spring of 1991 and the spring of 1992, we asked approximately 150 European managers attending courses at the International Institute for Management Development (IMD) in Lausanne, Switzerland to share with us their perceptions of American manufacturing competitiveness. The sample was not random and the methods were neither rigorous nor pristine, but the messages we got were loud and clear and, we think, insightful and important. The following summaries reflect the perceptions of the managers we spoke with.

Decision-Making Style.   *The American corporate decision-making style is, on balance, seen as a competitive advantage. The reasons for this are largely associated with the benefits (particularly time-wise) of innovative and entrepreneurial behavior and relatively high autonomy. There does appear to be, however, some contradictions between the expression of these characteristics and behaviors that might be more appropriate to a unifying Europe.*

European managers recognize the unusual success of American society in creating new technologies, giving birth to new industries. There is also thought to be a significant advantage in the U.S.'s being endowed with a large and homogeneous domestic market, where a pan-U.S. media exists for consumer education, where relatively homogeneous standards hold across the country, and where there is possibly less bureaucracy to be faced by a new business or a new idea. Yet the blessing is a mixed one.

American decision-making can also be characterized by the "fast-draw" cowboy, who shoots first and asks questions later. In Europe, with its heterogeneous population, the *process* by which a decision is made may well be as important (if not more so) as the decision itself. As an example, a case of restructuring a successful group of agricultural equipment manufacturers in anticipation of the coming pan-European market has typically been seen as an exercise in organizational geometry by American executives, who see nothing before them but the need to reconfigure and the intellectual puzzle of how to do it most efficiently. European executives, on the other hand, almost inevitably begin by lamenting and criticizing the insensitivity and haste of the responsible American-trained managers, as well as the style (or lack thereof) with which they make their decisions. For the Europeans, it is more the way the decisions were being made, rather than the decisions themselves, that focuses their attention and interpretation of the situation.

European managers are also weighing the attractiveness of American-inspired and currently fashionable decentralization initiatives against the often compelling opportunities to exploit significant economics of scale in the newly emerging pan-European market of 350 million consumers. In fact, there has often been a considerable degree of managerial autonomy in European operations, as a natural result of smaller and distinctive markets, tradition, and the historical role of the national firm. So while many American companies struggle with efforts to achieve flatter organizations to become more responsive, many European companies, in attempting to achieve the same objective, are finding themselves restructuring in such a way that more, not less, centralization in decision making is taking place.

Quite possibly, no one has ever tackled the contradictions between decentralization and the need/opportunity for greater coordination in as heroic a fashion as ABB, the merger resulting from Sweden's Asea and Switzerland's Brown Boveri, where activities are organized vertically by product into eight business segments, each responsible globally for organizing manufacturing units and product development and 59 business areas. Horizontally, the group is broken down into countries or regions (Dullforce 1991). According to CEO Percy Barnevik:

> ABB is a company with no geographic center, no national ax to grind. We are a federation of national companies with a global coordination center. Are we a Swiss company? Our headquarters is in Zurich, but only 100 professionals work at headquarters and we will not increase that number. Are we a Swedish company? I'm the CEO, and I was born and educated in Sweden. But our headquarters is not in Sweden, and only two of the eight members of our board of directors are Swedes. Perhaps we are an American company. We report our financial results in U.S. dollars, and English is ABB's official language. We conduct all high-level meetings in English. My point is that ABB is none of those things—and all of those things. We are not homeless. We are a company with many homes. (Taylor 1991).

Given the spectacular scale of ABB's experiment, there should be no surprise that it is prominently featured in the American business press. Yet the great success of the Swiss-based chocolate maker Jacobs Suchard Tobler, and indeed its attractiveness as an acquisition to Philip Morris, was, on the other hand, built on a strategy of *consolidation and recentralization.* Jacobs grew by acquiring the significant players in Europe's national chocolate markets (including some with international activities) and then restructuring them into focused manufacturing facilities, controlled by a central corporate core. Tobler, the venerable Swiss chocolate company, for example, went from being a complete product-line producer of fine chocolate to being a focused producer of Toblerone, the famous pyramid-shaped confection, for sale throughout Europe. In such cases, managerial autonomy was perceived as a competitive *disadvantage*, rather than an appropriate objective to be almost instinctively pursued.

Analytical Decision-Making Skills. *American managers are perceived as possessing advanced analytical decision-making skills—which, apparently, do them relatively little good in terms of ultimate market performance.*

The modern business school was born in the United States, and it has probably achieved its theoretical apogee there as well, with the unchecked spread of scholarly research, methodological rigor, and optimization techniques. Today in America it is not at all unusual to have a third successive generation of business school faculty in the classroom without any managerial experience at all. Alarming as this might seem, there is an inertia associated with such phenomenon that is even more insidious. It suggests the business schools are teaching the necessary topics even though the teachers may never have experienced the need for these topics. It suggests that the discipline-driven, functional structuring of the faculty in some way addresses the nonstructured, multidisciplinary issues that the audience needs addressed. And it suggests that if you break your problems down into easily defined boxes and optimize within those boxes, then everything will be optimal, or at least acceptable.

Whereas some European business schools are following the American model, many more are not. At IMD, for example, the emphasis is clearly not on optimization or academic theory, but rather on experiencing firsthand the process of decision making. Following Marshal McLuhan's aphorism that "the media is very often the message," IMD students are exposed to multi-cultural, multi-national, multi-language study groups in everything they do. An emphasis is also placed as much on the presentation of ideas and solutions as on the generation of these ideas and solutions. Finally, one of the *leitmotifs* that runs through the IMD educational experience is a continuing focus on the business system, or that series of institutional actors that populate the value chain and the interrelationships between them (Gilbert and Strebel 1986).

Short-term Profit Perspective. *It is quite clear that the short-term profit perspective of American corporations is perceived as a reality and a serious disadvantage for American manufacturing managers.*

In the report of MIT's Commission on Industrial Productivity, *Made in America* (Dertouzos et al. 1989), a very strong argument is made regarding the deleterious effects of a short-term business mentality among America's businesses:

We begin by describing a number of issues in which American firms have given ground to overseas competitors despite holding an early lead in technology or sales or both. In these instances it is reasonable to conclude that U.S. firms were less willing than their rivals to live through a period of heavy investment and meager returns in order to secure a foothold in a growing market. There may be cases in which the roles were reversed, but the evidence suggests that it is usually the Americans who are most concerned with near-term outcomes.

Clearly, and emphatically, our European managers agreed with this assessment.

Being able to move quickly and with great agility in the new global marketplace was seen by all as being absolutely necessary to survive in the future. The hesitancy of American firms to enter Eastern Europe was cited as an illustration of the inability of managers, who frequently know better, to be able to justify the long-term investments necessary in so many "difficult" markets and relationships. Consider, for a moment, the absolute eccentricity (from an American perspective) of Jean-Rene Fourtou, chairman of the French state-controlled pharmaceuticals and chemical company Rhone-Poulenc SA, when he states:

I live obsessed with the future, the vision, the priorities. To be effective, one must take a lot of time to dream about the future and to choose it. . . . Eventually, the company's ambition is to be an active industrial presence in all countries of the world. (Choi 1992)

Is Fourtou representative of most European managers? No, of course not. Europeans suffer from many of the same short-term tendencies that American managers do. In many countries, such as Germany and Switzerland, however, the short-term pressures that emanate from the equity markets simply do not exist in anywhere near the same degree that they do in the United States. In Germany, for example, the role of the banks is such that the firm is often buffered from many of the direct pressures from large institutional equity holders such as those existing in the U.S. Despite such structural explanations as to why certain managers are, or are not, more involved in long-range thinking, wouldn't it be great to work for someone who thought like Fourtou?

The odds are that longer-term investments, particularly those regarding high technology, are more likely to be supported in today's Europe than in the United States. Witness, for example, the following staggering statistic: "According to *American Machinist* magazine, the U.S. ranked 21st last year among industrial countries in the purchase of metalworking machine tools per capita last year—behind Romania" (Faltermayer 1991). We do not believe that such behavior would be acceptable among the aggressive European manufacturers we have been speaking with.

Technology. *There is little technological advantage conceded to American competitors, and, in fact, European technology is seen as often being of somewhat higher quality.*

Of course, the applicability of such opinions vary widely, from industry to industry. But underlying this generalization is the conviction that European technologies tend to exhibit greater precision and reliability, are arguably better made, and can be characterized by greater sturdiness. This may come as a shock to many American managers, who are quite assured that "Made in the USA" means, among other things, the *best* technology available. In fact, a relatively greater number of European firms appear to maintain a stronger commitment to technical tradition and craftsmanship than do their U.S. counterparts. Examples that have been offered to illustrate this opinion have included BMW and Mercedes-Benz—both in terms of the performance quality of their cars, and their initiative in pursuing "green manufacturing," and Volvo's reputation for building exceptionally safe vehicles.

There is a second facet of this perception of relative technology performance that American managers should also be familiar with. The above opinion also reflects a growing confidence that is building on such pan-European initiatives as EUREKA, a European-wide program (involving 19 countries) for joint corporate and university research on precompetitive projects in scientific and technical areas of high commercial potential; ESPRIT, a pan-European program

on fundamental and applied research in information technologies; JESSI, the Joint European Submicron Silicon Initiative; EFA, the European Fighter Aircraft project; Airbus Industrie; and the European Space Program. This says that Europe is not ready to be counted out of the international technology game. In fact, these consortia, though experiencing the ups and downs associated with large multinational high-technology cooperative projects, have had some rather spectacular successes, not the least of which has been Airbus, which has managed to win a significant amount of market share in the world airline business (formerly dominated by Boeing and McDonnell Douglas) and respect for its technologies.

R & D Commitment. *American managers are seen as being less committed to R&D than their European counterparts. Although this differs significantly by industry, the reasons for this perception appear to involve the relatively low investment levels in R&D that many American firms are making, and, again, a sense that American managers exhibit a willingness to trade R&D off against other variables.*

Perhaps what we are seeing here is another expression of the perception of American short-term thinking, yet the numbers in this case support the perceptions. American funding of R&D plateaued in the late 1980s, and now appears to be declining in the face of the prolonged recession and the end of the Cold War. At the same time, the R&D spending of its principal industrial competitors continues to increase. Clearly, of course, Americans are not seen as being alone in this regard. As an example, Phillips' decision in the fall of 1990 to withdraw from its role as leader in the development of a new generation of static random access memory (S-Ram) chips, as part of the $5 billion JESSI project, because of its financial difficulties at the time, was seen by some observers as threatening to "shrink the support base of the Netherlands for technological developments" (Skapinker and van de Krol 1990). Yet there is good reason for Americans to recognize the European commitment to process innovation and how that pays off in many competitive markets.

As an example, it is worthwhile recalling the great success Swiss manufacturers of precision equipment have had in overcoming the disadvantages of an expensive Swiss franc and an exceptionally high cost of labor. They have aggressively substituted capital for labor in their production processors while enhancing their reputation for high quality output. Of course, the challenge originated in the first place as a result of stiff immigration barriers that limited labor availability. The response of the industry was not to "cut and run" abroad, but to tackle the process in a serious and technically thoughtful manner. The Swiss watch industry was badly hurt in the 1970s when it failed to appreciate the power of product innovation as expressed by electronic watches. The great success of the Swatch, which has succeeded in making the wrist watch into an affordable fashion accessory, is also a testament to the ability of the Swiss industry to regroup and embark in new directions in a survival effort.

Design. *American industry really gets hammered on the design dimension. They are seen as being well behind Europe in terms of the perceived competitive importance and aesthetics of design.*

This should come as no surprise. Simply mention the word "Ferrari" and the message is clear. However, it is important for American managers to understand just how pervasive and significant the design dimension really is for European manufacturers. Alessi, for example, has transformed the everyday orange juice squeezer into both an art object and a best seller. The power of Dieter Ram's design concept, which makes any Braun product instantly recognizable, can even be seen as an influence in the Sensor, parent-company Gillette's flagship razor. The recent opening of several A/X Armani Exchange departments in three top American retailers— Bloomingdale's, Saks Fifth Avenue, and Neiman Marcus—again underlines how serious, and how successful, European manufacturers have been in using product design as a competitive advantage.

Nor is this perception a new one. The late Raymond Loewy, the foremost "American" designer of our times (although he was born in France), was featured on the cover of *Time* on October 31, 1949 as the man responsible for such designs as the Greyhound bus, the Coca-Cola fountain dispenser, the 1947 classic Studebaker design, the Avanti, the Shell Oil and Exxon logos, the interior of the Skylab space station, the redesign of Air Force 1, the Heinz and Nabisco logos, and the redesign of the Lucky Strike

package. In an interview with Peter Mayer in the late 1970's, he expressed his astonishment over America's failure to develop its design capabilities:

> To put it briefly, I was amazed at the chasm between the excellent quality of much American production and its gross appearance, clumsiness, bulk, and noise. Could this be the leading nation in the world, the America of my dreams? I could not imagine how such brilliant manufacturers, scientists, and businessmen could put up with it for so long. (Loewy 1988)

Quality. *American managers are perceived as not being totally committed to superior quality performance. It appears that this is seen not so much as being naive or misinformed as much as it is an issue of the likelihood of American managers—"in the end, when the chips are down"—to trade quality off against some other competitive variable. Incidentally, European managers, in self-reflection, do not come off very well compared to Japanese managers in this regard.*

Of course, everybody knows how important quality is for competitive success. And, of course, everyone is working hard to improve quality. But for many European managers, the current American pursuit of quality does not come across as being totally sincere. However, we believe the real meaning of this opinion has more to do with perceptions of performance than with conformance. What we were hearing was that with too many American product offerings, the performance of the product was simply not remarkable. Groupe Bull's perception of Zenith's personal computers as "aging and dull" after buying the American PC line says this as well as anyone (Hudson 1991).

It is on perceptions of product quality, based on performance, that such long-standing successes of European marques as Stihl and Hasselblad have been built. Conformance, in such products, is taken for granted: it is product character that makes the difference!

Manufacturing Practices. *European managers see American manufacturers as being relatively inflexible, largely because of their infatuation with large-scale manufacturing economies, old plants and equipment,* *significant inflexible backward integration, and a relatively low level of status and influence among the manufacturing function managers. There seems to be a strong notion of American manufacturing as a decidedly non-strategic practice.*

The MIT Commission on Industrial Productivity has expressed this perception as well as anyone:

The decline of the U.S. economy puzzles most Americans. The qualities and talents that gave rise to the dynamism of the postwar years must surely be present still in the national character, and yet American industry seems to have lost much of its vigor. In looking for ways to reverse the decline, it is only natural to turn to the methods that succeeded in the golden years of growth and innovation. . . . In industry after industry the [MIT] Commission's studies have found managers and workers so attached to the old way of doing things that they cannot understand the new economic environment. . . . The industry studies reveal two main elements of past practice that are impeding progress today. First is the reliance on mass production of standard commodity goods. (Dertouzos et al. 1989).

Northern Italy is often put forth as an example of the sort of manufacturing flexibility that is possible even in smaller firms who are able to adapt to sophisticated machinery. One of the great success stories of this region has been the ability of Mandelli S.p.A. to beat much larger rivals, such as the German Huller-Hille and the Japanese Yamazaki, in supplying the manufacturing capabilities necessary to make Volvo a truly flexible manufacturer. At Mandelli, the director of planning, Filippo Impellizzeri, observed. "The main obstacle to achieving our strategic goals is our size. We are not large enough (and when I talk about size I mean all aspects—people, technological domain, and financial mass) to leverage the company in geographic and application markets."

One of the solutions to this dilemma was the dedication of the firm to what was called Total Solutions Management. According to its president, Gian Carlo Mandelli:

We need to establish a relationship involving the closest collaboration [with our customers], be-

cause our customers, who want us to solve their production problems, must make us party to their technology. The result is that our know-how meshes with theirs through a sort of technological *joint venture*. It's an exchange between us—producer of the technology—and them—the users—with the benefit for us even greater than the value of the contract.

Such behavior is a far cry from the lament featured in the MIT report quoted at the beginning of this section. The old ways simply will no longer work, and mass production is among the greatest traps for everyone but those market leaders who can successfully distribute and sell mass merchandising items.

Sourcing. *In general, European manufacturers are thought to have better and somewhat more flexible sourcing relationships, particularly within Europe, as a result of their being more cosmopolitan and having longer-term perspectives.*

The key to understanding this perception goes back, we think, to the greater ease with which Europeans move across national and cultural boundaries, and the consequently greater facility for dealing with multicultural, multilingual, organizational combinations.

To some extent, the geography of Europe makes such activities considerably more natural. At Benetton, cultural norms regarding the nature of collaborative arrangements made it possible for the company to structure a cottage-industry supply system, owned by Benetton managers, that not only provided exceptional and low-cost manufacturing flexibility, but also created a win-win supply situation out of what in the U.S. would have been treated as a cut-and-dried instance of conflict of interest.

Perhaps nowhere is European industry's ability to coordinate multicultural activities more evident than in the opening up of Eastern and Central Europe. The speed and ease of West German firms moving into the former German Democratic Republic, the widespread West European activity in Czechoslovakia and Hungary, and the relatively great European presence in the republics of the former Soviet Union are all testimony to this attribute.

Education and Labor. *The American work force is clearly perceived to be a significant competitive liability. One very important reason for this is the low level of basic education. The American work force is also perceived as being relatively less skilled and less motivated than their European counterparts. In addition, there are fewer institutional remedies (such as apprenticeship programs or corporate loyalty) available to counter this phenomenon.*

Nowhere were the European managers we spoke with more concerned about America's long-range potential than with matters relating to education and labor force quality. Many of them had had firsthand experience with American factories, partners, or suppliers who were unable to implement JIT, statistical process control, or even elementary steps towards greater worker empowerment, because the American workers involved had too low a level of education to be able to perform the necessary tasks, take responsibility, or make informed decisions.

Furthermore, unlike some countries in Europe—Germany, for example, where there are 610,000 apprentices working in industry (Marsh 1991)—America was seen to have too little invested in the appropriate training and preparation of its work force. Nor did our European managers feel that the American workers they were familiar with had sufficient pride in their position to really act as a competitive asset. With regard to this latter point, one cannot help but be impressed with the way in which many European workers take a great deal of professional pride in their jobs—far beyond what is true in the United States.

However, the quality of life for European workers may well be so much better in some industries that it becomes a competitive liability. In Germany, for example, the average German automobile worker works approximately 1,700 hours per year, a number that is set to drop to 1,600 hours in 1994. Their American counterparts at General Motors work 2,000 hours per year; at Toyota, in Japan, the average is 2,300 hours per year:

> Generally, Europe's auto workers get five or six weeks of paid vacation a year, receive virtually free health care and college educations for their children, and, more and more, own the house or apartment in which they live. (Aeppel 1992)

In Europe, language, work permits, and the like have created barriers to labor mobility that will only be reduced, not removed, with the opening up of the post-1992 Economic community. In addition, the "greying" of Europe's population, and growing concerns over the numbers of guest workers in many countries, will make domestic labor an increasingly scarce resource. One result of all of this is that labor is seen more as a fixed cost by European managers than appears to be the case with their American counterparts. In some ways, therefore, European firms appear to be somewhat more experienced in dealing with issues regarding the screening, acquisition, deployment, and retention of labor.

To plumb the perceptions of one continent about the strengths and weaknesses of another is a difficult and dangerous thing to attempt. All societies have strengths and weaknesses, but often the perceptions of outsiders provide a different view than that typically held by the inhabitants being examined. In this way there is a great opportunity for learning. In summing up their perceptions of America, our European managers attempted a grand synthesis, which in effect said:

> American society is seen as being open, dynamic, and rich in the sorts of characteristics that lead to risk taking, entrepreneurship, creative vitality, and hard work. American society is seen as being plagued by a variety of social problems, malaise, and an undervaluation of manufacturing that leads to its strengths not paying off in a competitive manufacturing sense.

Although much of what was related above appeared critical, such was not the actual tenor of most of the actual discussions. In truth, the great majority of the European managers we spoke held American society in a great deal of respect and even admiration. America was seen to be a society of great vitality and creativity, with well-meaning beliefs and a large and skilled pool of talent. To be fair, though, almost all the European managers preferred the quality of life associated with living in Europe. This love-hate relationship was best articulated by Carlo De Benedetti, who when asked what for him was the ideal life, replied, "Working in America, sleeping in Italy" (Krause 1991).

Yet another dominant feeling about America that appears particularly important in our discussions with European managers was *mystification*. Consistently, the Europeans were mystified about how America had allowed itself to get into the terrible competitive position it is now in. Rather than being gleeful or condescendingly smug, the European managers expressed sympathy and regret for the decline of a society they had respected for quite some time. Unable to avoid the ever-present declining fortunes of so many American industries, and in the wake of President Bush's trip to Japan earlier this year, to the Europeans the question remains: "To where, and why, have America's industrial leaders disappeared?"

References

Timothy Aeppel, "In Europe's Car Plants, Pay Is High and Hours Are Few." *The Wall Street Journal Europe.* February 27, 1992, p.8

Jacques Attali, *Millennium* (New York, Random House, 1991).

William J. Broad, "U.S. Research Spending Peaks, and Rivals Sprint to Close the Gap," *International Herald Tribune*, February 22–23, 1992, pp. 1, 5.

Audrey Choi, "Fourtou Boosts Rhone-Poulenc Presence," *The Wall Street Journal Europe*, February 21–22, 1992, p.9

Michael L. Dertouzos, Richard K. Lester, and Robert M. Solow, *Made In America* (New York: Harper-Perennial, 1989).

William Dullforce, "First the Creation—But the Fruits Have Still To Be Fully Realised," *The Financial Times.* April 5, 1991, p. 29.

Edmund Faltermayer, "U.S. Companies Come Back Home," *Fortune*, December 30, 1991, pp. 88–92.

C. Michael Farr and William A. Fischer, "Managing International High Technology Cooperative Projects," *R&D Management*, January 1992, pp. 55–67.

Xavier Gilbert and Paul Strebel, "Developing Competitive Advantage," in William D. Guth (ed.) *Handbook of Business Strategy: 1986-1987 Yearbook* (Boston: Warren, Gorham and Lamont, 1986).

Bernard K. Gordon, "Myths of America's Trade Balance with Europe," *The Wall Street Journal Europe*, January 10–11, 1992, p. 6.

David P. Hale, "Learning from Germany and Japan." *The Wall Street Journal Europe*, February 5, 1991. p. 8.

Richard L. Hudson, "Groupe Bull Unveils a Revitalized Zenith," *The Wall Street Journal Europe*, May 17–19, 1991, p. 10.

Cathy B. Huycke and Michael D. Oliff, *Mandelli SpA.* (A–D), IMD cases, September–November 991.

Axel Krause. *Inside the New Europe* (New York: Harper Collins, 1991).

Robert E. Lipsey. NBER working paper No. 3293, as quoted in Lindley H. Clark, "Europe '92 is Mostly a Break for Americans." *The Wall Street Journal Europe*, June 1–2, 1990. p. 6.

Raymond Loewy, *Industrial Design* (Woodstock, N.Y.: The Overlook Press, 1988).

David Marsh, "A Hard Act for Britain to Follow," *The Financial Times*, April 15, 1991. p.12.

Richard A. Melcher, Patrick Oster, and Steward Toy, "Europe, Too, Is Edgy About Imports—From America," *Business Week*, January 27, 1992. pp. 48–49.

Kenichi Ohmae, *Triad Power* (New York: The Free Press, 1985).

Michael Skapinker and Ronald van de Krol, "The Leading Light Goes Out," *The Financial Times*, September 5, 1990, p. 21.

William Taylor, "The Logic of Global Business: An Interview with ABB's Percy Barnevik," *Harvard Business Review*, March–April 1991, pp. 91–105.

Sandra Vandermerwe and Michael D. Oliff, "'Strategies for the '90s Mean Full Green Ahead,' Say Top Executives." *IMD Perspectives for Managers*, No. 1, 1991.

James P. Womack, Daniel T. Jones, and Daniel Roos, *The Machine that Changed the World* (New York: Rawson Associates, 1990).

Robert S. Collins is a professor of manufacturing management at the International Institute for Management Development (IMD) in Lausanne Switzerland.

William A. Fischer is also a professor of manufacturing management at IMD, and is the Dalton L. McMichael, Sr. Professor of Business Administration at the Kenan-Flagler Business School, University of North Carolina at Chapel Hill.

CASE STUDY: ISSUES IN CROSS-CULTURAL ADVERTISING

Background

There has been an active debate in the field of marketing since the mid-1960s about whether multinational companies can standardize rather than individualize their advertising for each country in which they market their products. According to Whitelock and Chung, "The controversy centers around whether common advertising themes or even the same advertisements with proper translations are as effective as separate messages and advertisements developed specifically for individual national markets."[3]

Some theorists believe that consumers' needs or wants are the same regardless of which country they call home, and because of this a multinational company can use the same advertisements, or very similar advertisements, for all of their markets. This, of course, appeals to companies trying to achieve economies of scale in their promotion, and the argument is particularly attractive to the smaller firms that have recently internationalized their markets.

---

[3] Jeryl Whitelock and Djamila Chung, "Cross-Cultural Advertising: An Empirical Study," *International Journal of Advertising,* 8, no. 3 (1989): 292.

At the other extreme of this argument are those who insist that advertisements must always be individualized for each country for the same product, pointing to the many differences among cultures and citing the numerous high-profile blunders made by firms when marketing to other countries.

Both these positions tend to take an all-or-nothing attitude toward standardized versus individualized advertisements. Actually, the problem is more complex. As Boddewyn, Soehl, and Picard demonstrated in their research on the European Economic Community, advertising is more resistant to standardization than products or brands.[4] Later research has shown that standardization versus individualization is dependent on several factors, including product type, the degree of homogeneity among markets, the degree to which a culture is high or low context, and how oriented the cultures are to individuals rather than groups.

One of the primary determinants of whether a firm can standardize its advertising is the amount of "cultural distance" between the firm's target markets. The concept of cultural distance was developed by Samover, Porter, and Jain to indicate relative similarity between the communication styles of different cultures.[5] According to the findings in this research, the more dissimilar two cultures are, the greater the need to individualize advertising. The variable of high-involvement versus low-involvement products thus becomes important in the decision of how standardized an advertisement should be. A high-involvement product in any culture requires more detailed information because the level of perceived risk is higher for these products. The need to impart more detailed information in one's advertisements increases the risk of making cultural blunders when using standardized advertisements.

The concept of cultural distance exists on a continuum. Therefore, a firm marketing to two fairly similar cultures, like the United States and Australia, might have no problem using the same advertisement for a low-involvement product. The same firm marketing a high-involvement product may have to make only minor changes in its advertisement. Researchers have shown that many of the same/similar advertisements used across cultures were primarily confined to "reminder" advertisements for well-known companies or brand names.

In their article, Whitelock and Chung developed a method for evaluating the degree of advertising standardization; it includes such considerations as:

- Was the same picture used in both advertisements?
- Were the advertisements the same size?
- Were different colors used?
- Were different layouts used?
- Were the captions different?
- Were there differences in the texts?

---

[4] J. J. Boddewyn, R. Soehl, and J. Picard, "Standardization in International Marketing: Is Ted Levitt Right?" *Business Horizons*, vol. 29 (November–December 1986): 72.

[5] L. Samovar, R. Porter, and N. Jain, *Understanding International Communication* (Belmont, CA: Wadsworth, 1981), 29.

- Was the advertisement translated into another language?
- Did the translation have the same meaning?[6]

Instructions: For this exercise in content analysis of advertisements, the authors contacted Godiva Chocolatiers, makers of prestige-priced, high-quality chocolate candy. Godiva's headquarters is in Brussels, Belgium, but the product is sold all over the world. Godiva U.S.A. sent six advertisements and Godiva Japan sent five advertisements. (Godiva is distributed in Japan by Campbell Foods Japan.) All these advertisements ran in print media in their respective countries during 1992 or 1993.

Not all the advertisements from each country are reproduced in your text, but the following chart gives you a breakdown of all the ads by theme and occasion:

Theme/Occasion	American	Japanese
Valentine	Yes	Yes
Christmas	Yes	Yes
Easter	Yes	No
Thank you	Yes	No
Gift to friends	Yes	No
Birthday	Yes	No
Nostalgia for classmates	No	Yes
Nostalgia/early romance	No	Yes

Study the advertisements and answer the following questions:

1. Based on a comparison of these ads, what general conclusions can you state about the two cultures?

2. Why do you think Godiva used different advertisements in the two countries?

3. Enumerate and explain in cultural terms the differences you see in the ads.

The following are the translations of the advertising copy for the Japanese Godiva advertisements:

1. *Christmas tree ad:* "A cold northerly wind, a warm room, the sound of the singing of hymns somewhere, the flickering of a candlelight—that Godiva Tryufam."

2. *Dancing couple ad:* "The melody then, three years ago today, a pavement as the rain is letting up, an encore for the couple—that Godiva Carle."

3. *Planter (for Valentine's Day) ad:* "A telephone number that (he/she) has never called before, the pounding of the heart, awkward words, the beginning of a relationship—that Godiva Heartmilk."

---

[6] Whitelock and Chung p. 301.

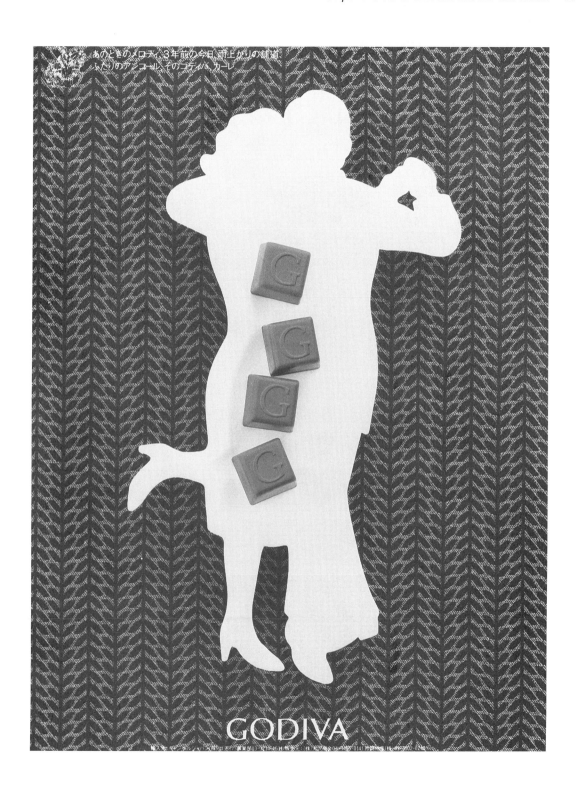

SUGGESTED READINGS

Fabrikant, Geraldine. "Many Readers, Few Ads for Bauer." *New York Times*, 22 May 1991, D1:3.

Kanso, Ali. "International Advertising Strategies: Global Commitment to Local Vision." *Journal of Advertising Research* 32, no. 1 (February 1992): 71–73.

Levitt, Theodore. "The Globalization of Markets." *Harvard Business Review* 61, no.3 (May/June 1983): 92–102.

Monk-Turner, Elizabeth. "Comparing Advertisements in British and American Women's Magazines, 1988–1989." *Sociology and Social Research* 75, no. 1 (October 1990): 53–57.

GLOBAL MARKETING: EXPERTS LOOK AT BOTH SIDES

Keith Reinhard

Keith Reinhard, chairman and chief executive officer of Needham Harper Worldwide, New York, spoke about global marketing at a meeting of the Atlanta Advertising Club in January. The following is an edited version of his remarks.

"We are taking the business of global marketing so seriously that we recently changed our name to Nedham Harper Worldwide to acknowledge our commitment to that very thing. In fact, it's such a new name, not everyone in the world knows it yet. As for our global view or at least mine, I, for one, believe there will be more global brands (in the future) than there are now—probably quite a few more. I've heard all the arguments about how global marketing is overrated because there are only about three global brands—Coke, McDonald's, and Kodak.

"Even if that were true, which it isn't, as global media continue to open global markets, it will surely follow that companies all over the world will find ways to create and market ever-increasing numbers of new global brands.

"But if you ask me, the biggest impediment to successful global marketing may prove to be 'turf.'

"Most of us experience it now within our own country. You know—if it wasn't invented by the Detroit office it won't work in Detroit. And what may be great in New York won't work in Chicago. And just because it's an effective strategy in the U.S., don't expect it to play in Canada. Recognize it? Turf. Not invented here. Territorial rights. The animals are not alone in defending them to the death. This problem exists both within agencies and client organizations. It has to be whipped before we can truly market globally.

Reprinted with permission from the April 15, 1985 issue of *Advertising Age.* Copyright, Crain Communications, Inc., 1985.

"But with all this, whatever problems continue to nag at us—cultural, national, territorial—I don't believe they are going to be creative problems. Speaking for the creative community, I feel confident in saying to would-be global marketers, 'creative is ready when you are,' to paraphrase Delta's time-honored pledge to us.

"What it boils down to is that we are all human. We share the gift of emotional response. We feel things. And we feel them in remarkably similar ways. We speak different languages, we observe different customs, but we are wired to each other and to an ultimate power source that transcends us in a way that makes us subject to a common emotional spectrum."

W.E. Phillips, chairman of the Ogilvy Group, does not share Keith Reinhard's views on global marketing. Here is an edited excerpt of his remarks to the British-American Chamber of Commerce in March.

"When we assume that because the Americans and the British share some common heritage and a common political purpose, all differences are minor—that we understand each other really rather well—we are led astray.

"In fact, the minor differences in our use of language conceal major differences in our approaches to life. And if these differences are large between us, think of the gaps that exist between nations with less common cultures and no common language at all.

"Multinational companies often look for efficiencies. They long to treat personnel the same way all over the world, believing that all people are much the same and that what works in the U.S. will work elsewhere. Thought to the contrary is often discounted as national pride. But when businesses do not recognize national cultural differences, they can't be as effectively run as those that do. The cultural connection counts, though it takes much more time and energy.

"We Americans tend to be direct. Indeed, the British are often shocked by that directness, shocked by how quickly we ask questions about money and personal lives. We tend to get straight to the issue and, on the whole, we say what we mean.

"The British, by contrast, rarely say what they mean in a flat-footed way. Americans are amenable to the direct sell, they like to be sold. The British don't even want to *mention* money, and they don't want to be told what to do by *anybody*.

"We have to *celebrate* the differences, not *dismiss* them. We cannot always choose the simplistic, efficient approach. Rather, we can use global product and advertising strategies, but the execution should be tailored to the specific market for maximum effectiveness.

"World brands are great commercial properties which need worldwide strategies and effective executions tailored to market needs. The successful marketers today know that a lot of perspiration and perspective is key to commercial success. Superficial impressions without cultural understanding usually lose to the dedicated competitor who takes the time to be right in every market."

CASE STUDY: BLANCHWORTH CHINA CASE

The Blanchworth China Company was founded in the British Isles in the eighteenth century and has established a worldwide reputation for premium quality china designed and handcrafted in the United Kingdom. The china always has sold very well in the United States and in the early 1980s, fueled by a strong dollar, it experienced an explosive growth in sales. However, as the dollar went into a long decline through the mid- and late 1980s, sales of Blanchworth china dropped by 25 percent in the United States. This decline is particularly important to Blanchworth since the U.S. market accounts for approximately 90 percent of the company's output.

The premium quality china market is roughly divided into two segments based on price: The high segment is priced from US $75 to US $300 per plate, while the lower segment ranges from US $25 to US $75 per plate. Blanchworth has always dominated the high segment with approximately 85 percent market share, but the company had no presence in the lower segment. Unfortunately, it was the high segment of the market that decreased 25 percent in sales dollars in the late 1980s, while the lower segment had grown by 50 percent during the same period. This was clearly a worldwide trend, not only in Blanchworth's market, but also for most other discretionary income items.

In addition to the falling value of the U.S. dollar and the shrinking market for higher-priced china, several other factors helped to create a severe financial crisis for Blanchworth by the end of the 1980s. During the "good times" of the 1980s, when demand and profits

were high, Blanchworth's skilled workers union made heavy wage and work-rule demands. The company's managers acceded to these demands in order to avoid any work stoppages. As a result, Blanchworth's craftsmen became some of the highest paid skilled workers in the British Isles. Workers' salaries increased from 60 percent of the cost of product to nearly 80 percent by the late 1980s. These high labor costs, coupled with company debt incurred by the acquisition of a premium crystal manufacturer, prevented Blanchworth from lowering its prices when U.S. demand decreased.

In 1988, management was forced to propose immediate cost-reducing measures in order to save the company. Among other things, they determined to reduce their labor force by 25 percent and to purchase new equipment that would make the remaining workers more productive. After heated encounters between management and union leaders, the union finally became convinced that the labor force cuts were necessary in order to save the company. The union also agreed to rescind work rules that had worked to preclude higher worker productivity. The union made these concessions in order to prevent the company from declaring bankruptcy and to save most union jobs.

After a year of operation with the new equipment, Blanchworth management found that increases in productivity were offset by the larger than expected number of senior craftsmen taking advantage of the early retirement package. This package was offered as one means of reducing the labor force by the targeted 25 percent. Profits continued to slide after the work force reduction, and Blanchworth management finally decided the company would have to enter the lower segment of the premium quality china market. While Blanchworth managers realized that there are many more competitors in this lower segment of the market than in the high-price segment, they believed the company's well-respected name and other marketing strengths would allow it to make a quick entry into this segment.

In late 1990, Blanchworth introduced a new line of products that is lighter in weight and less ornate than its original china place settings. This entire product line is produced in Eastern Europe at a fraction of the labor cost associated with the Blanchworth U.K. plant. Preliminary market research shows that this line has stronger appeal for the younger, first-time china buyers who see themselves as more contemporary and value-conscious than traditional Blanchworth customers; moreover, these younger buyers are generally less brand loyal. Blanchworth calls its new line *Krohn China*.

Krohn is carried by the same distribution channel as Blanchworth, but it has its own logo, package design, advertising agency, and display case. Management felt that the name Blanchworth associated with the name Krohn would help to establish an image of high quality, but, at the same time, the name Krohn would differentiate the new line from traditional Blanchworth china. This name association has helped to gain the reseller support necessary in making the new line readily accessible to a large market.

As a result of Blanchworth management's decision to locate its new operations in Eastern Europe, members of the union and residents of the community in which the Blanchworth factory is located feel betrayed. Union leaders were never informed about the new product line that could have meant the rehiring of many Blanchworth skilled workers. In addition, the move to Eastern Europe has caused ill-will among many consumers throughout the United Kingdom and has resulted in some critical editorial articles in the local and national press.

The union contends that most American customers are brand loyal to Blanchworth because it is made by skilled workers in the United Kingdom. They argue that this loyalty stems from the fact that many Americans trace their ancestry to one or more countries in the United Kingdom. Management counters that Blanchworth has never been sold specifically as a U.K. product and that most American buyers neither know nor care where their china products are made. Although there were many bitter feelings between management and the union, there were no work stoppages during 1991.

In early 1992, management announced that after the first year of sales Krohn generated twice as much profit per plate as Blanchworth. Also, they asserted that Blanchworth employees in the United Kingdom were still not productive enough to offset the high wages these workers earned. As a result, management representatives opened discussions with union leaders about how to solve the continuing low-profit problem. Management suggested that the only solution was a further reduction in wages and benefits, as well as another major change in work rules. The union disagreed with this perspective and countered that the low level of profitability actually resulted from poor management, rather than "overpaid, unproductive workers" as suggested by management.

While never openly stated, union leaders suspect that management may be considering moving all Blanchworth operations to Eastern Europe. The union continues to argue that U.S. customers will not accept Blanchworth china that is not made by U.K. craftsmen. They cite the fact that 100,000 tourists tour the U.K. plant each year and that at least half of these tourists are Americans. Many of these American tourists purchase over US $1,000.00 in china products during their visit to the plant. The union contends that the tourists who come to the plant feel a strong affinity for Blanchworth china because it is a product of the United Kingdom, and that most of these on-site sales would be lost if the plant were moved to Eastern Europe. To further strengthen this argument, the union cites the U.S. Census Bureau 1990 statistics giving the following breakdown of U.S. citizens by U.K. ancestry: England 32.6 million, Scotland 5.4 million, Ireland 38.7 million, and Wales 2.0 million.

Instructions: You are a business consultant who has been brought in to assist Blanchworth's top management with strategic decision making in several areas. During the briefing you are given additional information:

- Management is seriously considering moving all Blanchworth factory operations to Eastern Europe while keeping its other functions in the United Kingdom. They make it clear that the design and quality assurance operations would remain in the United Kingdom. There is concern about how quickly the new Eastern European plant and workers could achieve full quality production, especially if the U.K. workers shut down the British plant before the new plant is on line.

- Management is concerned about political instability in Eastern Europe. If they move both Krohn and Blanchworth, their entire production could be compromised and there would be little chance of reopening a plant in the United Kingdom.

- Sales of Krohn in the United Kingdom are extremely sluggish, but are doing well on the continent. Krohn does seem to be gaining acceptance slowly in the United

States, mostly among young couples buying it for themselves rather than receiving it as gifts from parents or friends and relatives.

■ The union and the community have threatened to discredit the firm if it moves to Eastern Europe by taking their case directly to the United Kingdom and United States customers.

Answer the following questions about this case:

1. The management believes its foreign sales will be unaffected by moving all operations to Eastern Europe. What research should be done before making this decision? Which research methodology do you recommend?

2. Is fine china considered by most people to be a functional piece of household ware? Or is it more a work of art with an artist and a history which are "value-added" to the physical product? Which research methodology will you use to find the answer to this question?

3. Try to anticipate the ways in which the union and the community could discredit the company name if it leaves the United Kingdom. Will Americans boycott the company *after* the move? Will Americans voice their disapproval in large numbers *before* the move? How will you get these answers?

4. What specific measures can management take to "inoculate" the firm against the union actions that you anticipated in Question 3? Should it do this rather than dealing with the problem after it is a reality?

5. Should management ask for concessions in order to keep the firm in the United Kingdom? Make a list of possible concessions and tell who should provide them, for example, the union, community, national government, and so on. Concentrate on the long-term solutions when sketching out a plan for how a win/win situation can be reached in this case.

CASE STUDY: SOUTHWESTERN MANUFACTURING COMPANY

Judith Vincent pulled the trailer into the parking lot of the Loew's Anatole Hotel in Dallas and sighed with relief that her long journey was over. The trailer was packed with samples of drums and lampshades from her factory in Lobos City, New Mexico, and Judith was hopeful that she would get many substantial orders for these items during the next three days at the Southwestern art and furniture show at the World Trade Center.

Judith went into the hotel lobby and gave the clerk her room reservation number. As he called up the reservation on his computer, he said, "Mrs. Vincent, I have a message here for you to call your husband as soon as you arrive." Judith thought, "That's odd; Ken doesn't usually leave messages like that. Oh, well, he probably just wants to know that I've arrived safely. I'll call him when I get to my room."

After the bellhop delivered her luggage, Judith sat down at the desk in her room and dialed her home number in Lobos City. Finally, after many rings, her six-year-old daughter, Amy, answered the phone. "Hi, honey. It's Mommy," Judith said. "Is Daddy there?"

"No, Mommy. He's at the fire. It's burning down and all the drums are gone! There are trucks and sirens everywhere. I'm scared! Come home, Mommy!"

Judith forced aside her initial panic. She said, much more calmly than she felt, "It's going to be all right, Amy. Let me talk to your grandmother. Is she there?"

"She's not here. She's looking for Oliver. She heard him barking but she can't find him."

Momentarily, Judith wanted to shout out her panic. What was Amy talking about? And why weren't Ken and her mother with Amy? "Who is with you, Amy? Who's taking care of you?" Judith finally managed to ask.

"Stacy's here," Amy sobbed.

Finally, after what seemed like an eternity, Stacy, the girl who lived next door and who occasionally took care of Amy, came on the phone. "Hello, Mrs. Vincent. This is Stacy. I'm so sorry."

"What is going on, Stacy? Where is everyone? What did Amy mean about a fire?" Judith shouted into the phone, no longer able to hide her growing alarm.

"The factory is on fire, Mrs. Vincent. Everyone is down there trying to put it out. It just keeps burning and burning. Mr. Vincent said to tell you to come home as soon as you called."

Judith sat back in her chair and was silent, stunned by the enormity of what Stacy had just told her. Finally, she said, "All right, Stacy. Tell Ken I'm on my way. I'll be there as soon as I can."

Later that evening, on the 650-mile drive from Dallas to Lobos City, Judith began to realize what she was going back to. All that she and Ken had worked for during the last three years was in flames. The business that they had struggled to keep going was about to disappear. And as this reality began to take shape in her mind, Judith thought back over their efforts during those three years and wondered if they would ever have the desire to rebuild.

The drum factory she and Ken had bought three years ago manufactured authentic Native American drums, as well as lampshades made from the same hides. Their 15 employees represented the three ethnic groups who make up the population of northern New Mexico: Pueblo Indians, Hispanics, and Anglos. The factory itself comprised 10,000 square feet, including the storage area where the hollowed-out logs used for the bodies of the drums were left to cure for 10–12 months.

As Judith imagined the factory, she saw each of the 14 on-site employees at their workstations. Three male Hispanic workers prepared the logs for the drum shells by cutting, sanding, and drilling holes in the sides for the rawhide laces. After these logs were thoroughly dried, the shells were transferred inside to Juan, Felipe, and Carlos, the principal drum makers and highest paid employees in the factory. Despite their Spanish surnames, all three were Native Americans and lived in Los Robles Pueblo[7]. Juan's sister, Anita, and Felipe's wife, Teresa, worked at tables close to the drum makers where the women assembled the lampshades. A third woman, Rosa, a Hispanic, also worked on the lampshades. In an adjacent room, Chris, an Anglo, and Jose, a member of the Pueblo, worked with the chemicals used in curing the hides. Three Anglo employees worked in a separate office area: Jim and Susan handled the tasks involved with packing and shipping the finished products, and Paula kept track of the accounts receivable and payable. (See the floor plan of the factory and storage area on the next page.)

---

[7] Los Robles is one of the two dozen or so pueblos of New Mexico. These pueblos are villages inhabited by groups of North American Indians. Many of the villages retain the social systems and community organizations the Spanish explorers found when they arrived in the sixteenth century.

FLOOR PLAN OF DRUM FACTORY

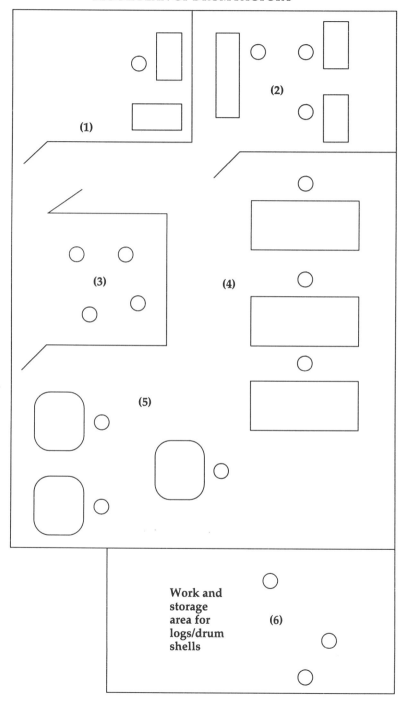

(1) **Ken's office**

(2) **Shipping and accounting office**

(3) **Area for curing hides**

(4) **Drum makers**

(5) **Lampshade makers**

Judith also recalled the many problems she and Ken had encountered during the last three years. In addition to marketing and distribution problems, they had faced numerous personnel difficulties. As she drove through the dark night across west Texas, Judith reviewed these problems in her mind.

First, productivity in the factory was lower than Ken and Judith thought it should be. Besides the three Native American drum makers, a fourth person—an Anglo woman named Marjorie—also made drums for the factory. Marjorie chose to work at home so that she could be with her small son, and she had agreed to work on a piecework basis rather than a salary. Her productivity was 15–20 percent greater than the productivity of the drum makers at the factory. Moreover, using the bonus point system that Ken had devised to compensate employees working on a piecework basis, Marjorie's income averaged 25 percent more than that of the Native American drum makers. When Ken had explained the bonus point system to Juan, Carlos, and Felipe, and offered them the opportunity to be compensated in this way rather than by a fixed salary, they had refused to consider it.

The work patterns and habits of the Native American employees were erratic, in comparison with how Ken and Judith expected employees to behave. Judith remembered how surprised she had been when none of the men from the Pueblo showed up for work one day in the late spring. When Ken asked Anita and Teresa why the men had not come to work, the women replied, "Oh, this is the week the men of the Pueblo irrigate the fields. They will be in the fields all week long." Later that year, the men were gone for another week during rabbit hunting season, although this time they had informed Ken of their impending absence.

Holidays were another problem. Judith had discovered that the Labor Day and Fourth of July holidays meant nothing to the Native American and Hispanic employees. Moreover, the Native Americans seemed irritated when the factory closed for the long Thanksgiving weekend. Both groups did observe Christian holidays like Easter and Christmas, and the Pueblo members observed some additional holidays that are part of the Native American religion. In fact, this month Juan was absent from the factory fulfilling his kiva[8] obligation. As he had explained to Judith, once every ten years the male members of the Pueblo were required to spend an entire month in the kiva participating in religious ceremonies and rites.

During the last three years, several employees had left the drum factory and set up their own small manufacturing companies, or they went to work for competing firms. Ken had decided it would be a good idea to ask new employees to sign a nondisclosure/noncompete contract, a standard practice in industries where a particular manufacturing process is the basis for a firm's success. In the large company where Ken had worked before buying the drum company, all employees were required to sign such a contract, and Ken modeled his contract on the one he had signed at International Products, Inc. However, when Ken presented the contract to the drum makers and other employees, he encountered stiff resistance from all of them; one drum maker had quit when Ken explained that signing the contract was a condition of employment. Ken finally abandoned this requirement when the others resisted his efforts.

---

[8] A kiva is a large, rectangular or circular, underground chamber used by Pueblo Indian men for religious ceremonies. The chamber has a fire pit in the center and is accessible by ladder. An opening in the floor of the kiva represents the entrance to the lower world and the opening through which life emerged into this world.

Ken knew that there were potential markets for other Native American artifacts, such as rattles and woven rugs, so he held a meeting last month with several of the employees to talk about manufacturing these new products. Because the drum makers often had free time between large orders, Ken thought that these employees could work on the other products. This would eliminate the need to hire additional employees to manufacture the rattles and rugs and thus would increase the company's productivity. Again, however, Carlos, Juan, and Felipe had refused to consider Ken's proposal, explaining that making rattles and weaving rugs were not things they would do. Ken decided not to pursue these new products until he could figure out why the drum makers were unwilling to cooperate. He knew that there had to be an explanation for the resistance to making rattles and rugs; perhaps when he discovered what that explanation was, he could figure out a way to deal with the employees' negative attitude.

There had been several instances of minor squabbles between the employees. Usually these involved the drum makers and one or two of the Hispanic women. None of these squabbles was serious or prolonged, but they contributed to an underlying tension among the workers. Just last week Judith had been in the factory when Rosa came into Ken's office complaining that Juan and Carlos were making fun of her. When Ken asked Rosa to tell him what had happened, she would only say, "I don't know what they were saying because they were speaking in Tewa, but I *know* that it was something bad about me." Ken had been in the middle of negotiating a contract for 1,500 lampshades with one of their European buyers and was unable to pursue the matter right away. Judith was uncertainabout what to do because Rosa's allegations were so nebulous. And Judith certainly didn't know how to confront Juan and Carlos about their actions because she didn't understand Tewa well enough to know exactly what they might have said to Rosa.

These minor confrontations between workers may have been one of the reasons Ken's efforts at encouraging teamwork had failed. He had attended a week-long seminar in Albuquerque for small business owners and one of the workshop topics had been "How to Establish and Maintain Teamwork among Your Employees." Ken came back to the factory with great enthusiasm for putting some of these techniques into practice and he began by combining the employees in small teams. The teams consisted of one person from each of the three areas involved in making the drums—the shell preparation stage, curing the hides, and the finishing work. After introducing the employees to some of the concepts from the seminar about how individuals can pool their talents and energies to create synergy, Ken asked the teams to discuss ways they could cooperate to increase their productivity and report back to him in a week.

During the first meeting all the employees had listened politely and Ken assumed that they understood the points he was making. When they came back together the following week, Ken asked one person from each team to tell the group what the team had discussed. No one had anything to say. Each team in turn had "passed" by saying that the group had not come up with any ideas on how to cooperate with each other. When Ken probed more specifically for what they had discussed, it became evident that the teams had not met together and so had not discussed anything.

At this point, Ken decided to appoint a leader for each group, rather than allowing leaders to emerge as he had hoped would happen when the employees got together for their discussions. This time he gave them a month to meet informally and he asked each appointed leader to report on the group's progress after two weeks. Unfortunately, Ken had had to go out of town for several days and he neglected to follow up on the groups' progress before the next meeting. At the end of the month, the employees got together again in Ken's office and the results were the same as before: no one had discussed team-work and cooperation. If anything, Ken sensed more animosity among the workers than before. He decided to drop the team concept temporarily until he could think through the problems of how to gain the support of each employee and of how to educate them about the team approach to problems.

About the time of Ken's last meeting, Judith had been making her plans for the trade show in Dallas. She wanted to take one or two of the drum makers to the trade show, but when she talked with Juan, Carlos, and Felipe about this, they all refused to go. She de-scribed the World Trade Center building in Dallas, with its myriad of booths, restaurants, stores, and other attractions, hoping that she could entice them by depicting the excitement of the crowds and the intensity of the big city as a contrast to the quiet little town of Lobos City. Judith thought that the drum makers would appreciate the opportunity to talk with people who admired the craftsmanship of the drums and who bought these works of art for the homes of clients all over the United States. Instead, the drum makers had been adamant in their refusal to accompany her on the trip. So Judith had gone to the trade show alone.

By the time Judith arrived back in Lobos City, the sun was up and the town's streets were filled with tourists. She turned off the main highway onto a narrow gravel road and steeled herself for what she would find three miles away. Even from here she could smell the acrid smoke and see the billows of black cloud rising from the debris of the factory. What would she and Ken do now? They had large backorders for both the drums and the lampshades, so the bank would probably be willing to lend them the money needed to rebuild. Moreover, the company had been consistently profitable with a lot of growth po-tential in both the domestic and foreign markets.

Should they rebuild and start over? she wondered. Or are the problems she had thought about on the trip home too great a deterrent?

Instructions:

1. Based on the material presented in the case study, what do you think are the main points of contention between the owners and the drum makers? What might be the reasons behind these problems, besides the specific reasons cited in the case study?

2. If you were a consultant hired by Judith and Ken to advise them on the personnel problems outlined in the case, how would you suggest they educate themselves regarding their employees? What do they need to know in order to be increas-ingly successful if they decide to rebuild after the fire?

SUGGESTED READINGS

Reno, Philip. *Taos Pueblo*. Chicago: Sage Books, 1972.

Wood, Nancy C. *Taos Pueblo*. New York: Knopf, 1989.

CASE STUDY: PRICING EXPORTS . . . THE HARD WAY

Tim Ballard looked out his office window at the mountains in the distance and thought about the phone call he had just received from Finland. One of Tim's best international customers, Olë Kulla, is a small wholesaler who travels throughout much of Scandinavia. Olë handles several lines of high-priced gifts, including the solar-powered executive gifts that Tim's company, Solar World, manufactures. Olë had called Tim today to see if Solar World would be interested in setting up a distribution network in Russia, Latvia, and Lithuania.

Tim's initial response to Olë's question was no. "Thanks for thinking of us," he told Olë, "but I don't think we're interested in trying to do business in Russia. We're too small a company to take that kind of risk and I don't have the manufacturing capacity to extend much beyond our present markets."

However, Tim listened carefully as Olë explained that Boris Ivanov, a Moscow entrepreneur whom Olë had met a year ago in Sweden, was looking for unusual gift items to sell in Russia, Latvia, and Lithuania. Boris, according to Olë, had established a sales network in the three former Soviet republics and was always looking for new products. Olë had shown Boris some of Solar World's executive gifts and Boris had expressed a strong interest in the products. He asked Olë to call Tim and set up a meeting, or at least a telephone conference to discuss the possibility of doing business.

"Boris has been extremely successful in setting up a business now that individuals can own businesses in the former Soviet Union. He seems to understand the free enterprise system very well," Olë told Tim. "I think it might be worth your time to talk with him about selling Solar World products in Russia."

Tim agreed to think over what Olë had said and to let him know if he wanted to contact Boris.

"The first thing I need to do," Tim thought after this telephone conversation, "is to get out the atlas and see where Lithuania and Latvia are located! I think I know where Russia is."

The next day Tim mentioned Olë's phone call to George Stephens, Solar World's sales manager. "I'm not convinced that this is something we want to pursue," Tim said, "but isn't it interesting that even a former Communist country might be interested in buying our executive gifts?"

"I wouldn't dismiss the Russian businessman's inquiry completely," George replied quickly. "I happened to be talking to Ben Rodriguez over at BR, Inc. yesterday, and he's just come back from a trip to Eastern Europe and Russia. He's planning to sell some of their specialty advertising items to Russia.

"Ben took a consultant with him when he went to Russia," George continued. "Maybe we ought to give her a call and see what's involved in doing business over there."

Later that week Tim did talk with Nina Churkin, the business consultant whom Ben Rodriguez recommended. Nina had been born and educated in the former Soviet Union; after she emigrated to the United States, she completed an MBA at an American university. She advised Tim that if he had any interest in doing business in Russia, he would have to go there in person to meet Boris Ivanov.

"It's very difficult to do business long-distance with anyone in Russia—their communication system is not as reliable and advanced as in the United States, and personal relationships are much more important in doing business there than in the United States," Nina told Tim. "Also, you need to be prepared to accept payment for your product in some form other than rubles or dollars."

"I don't understand," Tim said. "The firms I sell to in Finland and in Japan give me an international letter of credit and I receive payment through the bank. I never even have to convert from another currency."

Nina laughed. "Unfortunately, Russia and the other former Communist bloc countries don't have many hard currency reserves. They are relying heavily on countertrade for obtaining products from the West."

"Countertrade? I don't know what that is," Tim said.

"There are several forms of countertrade. The simplest is barter. That's where you trade Boris a certain number of your products in exchange for an agreed-upon number of one or more products produced in Russia. An example of a Russian good he might be able to obtain for trade would be *matroyshka* dolls, those colorfully painted, nesting dolls that children love. Or some companies have access to *shapka*, the distinctive fur hats many Russians wear."

"Dolls? Fur hats? What would I do with dolls or fur hats?" Tim asked. "I don't sell children's toys or clothing. That sounds like a crazy way to do business."

"Countertrade sometimes takes a different form than straight barter. I think another way of doing it is called a *buyback agreement*. In this situation, you would give Boris the technical information or specialized components he needs in order to make the executive gifts your company produces here. Then Boris produces those gifts in Russia and gives you a specified number on a regular basis as repayment for the technical information. You can sell those Russian-made gifts to your other customers, perhaps in Europe or back here in the United States."

"You mean I would sell our technical expertise to someone in Russia? How would I protect myself in that case? What would prevent him from using it and not paying me with finished goods?"

"Only a lawyer—and one familiar with Russian law as well as American law—can answer those questions. You do need to be concerned about those issues."

Tim was intrigued, although somewhat perplexed, by what Nina told him. Using a countertrade arrangement in Russia might just give him the potential to increase his production without incurring more debt. And if the finished products were already in Europe, he could eliminate the transportation costs he now had to build in when shipping from the United States.

Tim called his banker to find out more about countertrade. His banker's response was negative about doing business using countertrade.

"Those payment arrangements are fraught with problems," the banker said. "My advice is don't have anything to do with companies or individuals who propose countertrade. An irrevocable letter of credit is the only way you should be doing business in the international market."

Although the banker had been helpful on many occasions when Tim had needed an increase in his line of credit, Tim also realized that bankers tend to be very conservative about business transactions that eliminate the bank as a financial middleman. And since he knew that Ben Rodriguez at BR, Inc., was considering exchanging his company's finished goods for Russian-produced goods, Tim decided to regard his banker's advice as only one of many pieces to fit into what he was coming to regard as the countertrade puzzle.

Next, Tim contacted Lauren Kruph, a local attorney who was writing a comparative study of Russian and American legal systems. Lauren confirmed Tim's concerns that there were a number of potential legal problems involved in doing business in Russia, especially if he decided to use countertrade.

"The problems almost certainly can be resolved," Lauren said, "but you will need to contact a Russian lawyer as well as an American one. The process may be time-consuming and expensive. However, if this deal seems profitable enough in other respects, the legal expenses will be worth it."

After discussing the information obtained from Lauren, Nina, and the banker with his sales manager, they agreed that Tim should call Olë in Helsinki.

"I've decided to consider selling our products in Russia, Latvia, and Lithuania," Tim told Olë. "But first I want to suggest a possible deal between you and me. How about your buying the products from Solar World and then selling them to or countertrading them with Boris for some Russian products? That way, you can make a profit from this deal, too."

"I'm afraid my cash flow is not good enough for that kind of deal, Tim," replied Olë. "I already take some goods as countertrade for the Finnish and Swedish goods I sell Boris. Possibly I could take some Russian products, if Boris offers you the right ones in exchange for Solar World's products. But I can't directly buy your goods to sell or trade with Boris.

"I'm glad to know that you're anticipating the probability of a countertrade offer from Boris," Olë continued. "It's best if you're prepared to react to any of several different options he may suggest. Based on what Boris projects he can do with the markets he wants to open up to Solar World's goods, you could eventually double your annual sales. Why don't I set up a meeting for the two of you here in Helsinki and perhaps I can help with the negotiations."

Olë had been Tim's first international customer, and over the last six years had been a tremendous help in explaining the intricacies of doing business in Europe. Now Tim regarded Olë as a friend, as well as a customer, and he appreciated Olë's offer to meet with Boris.

Tim agreed to meet with Boris in Helsinki and began to review Solar World's current position in preparation for his trip.

Solar World is a small firm, employing fourteen assemblers to manufacture the company's various products, including the solar-powered executive gifts that Olë sells, solar-powered flashlights and battery packs, high-tech microsolar panels (on which the company has a monopoly), and educational solar kits. The company also employs three people in office and accounting jobs, plus George, the sales manager, and Tim, the company president. Solar World's annual sales are about $1.5 million; approximately 20 percent, or $300,000, of the sales are made in Europe and Japan.

The firm's offices and plant are in a small, one-story office building in Colorado Springs, Colorado. The rest of the building is occupied at the present time, so any expansion in production facilities would necessitate moving to another site.

As Tim reviewed Solar World's position, he suddenly remembered an inquiry from a German wholesaler that the company had received three months ago. The German firm wanted to represent the executive gift line in all parts of Europe south of Scandinavia where Olë had exclusive distribution rights. The German representative estimated that eventually he would be buying 10,000 units per month, perhaps as soon as six months after his initial purchase. Because of the large projected volume, which was several times the amount Olë sold now, the German wanted the product at a much lower price than Solar World sold them to the Finnish distributor. The German told Tim the end-user price he needed in order to move the projected volume, as well as the margin he would need in order to handle Solar World's products. Tim used these figures to work backwards when setting a price for the German. Unfortunately, he discovered that the transportation and tariff costs would not allow Solar World enough profit to do this deal with its present cost structure. Moreover, the higher volume would require a second production shift with all new employees and the many costs associated with those additional employees. Tim reluctantly had turned down this potential buyer. Now, however, with the possibility of obtaining finished products from a factory in Russia, Tim began to rethink his options regarding sales to the German firm.

Tim developed the following list of questions that he needs to answer before meeting with Boris:

1. What are some alternative proposals that Boris might suggest at the Helsinki meeting? Can some aspect of countertrade be used as the basis for each proposal?

2. What are the pros and cons of countertrade for a firm the size and complexity of Solar World?

3. If Solar World accepts one of the countertrade proposals, what are the company's resources for selling or trading the goods it receives? How would the company price these countertraded goods? How should the company price its own goods under the countertrade conditions?

4. If Solar World decides to sell the technology license to the Russian firm, what should be the price?

5. Which of the alternatives identified above is the best one for Solar World? Why?

Instructions:

1. Begin working on a solution to this case by reading the two articles, "New Trends in Countertrade" and "Countertrade as an Export Strategy," for some additional information about using countertrade in international business transactions. The authors of these two articles present two different views of the advantages and disadvantages of countertrade.

2. Look at the list of questions at the end of the case. How would you advise Tim in each area in preparation for the Helsinki meeting?

SUGGESTED READINGS

Bertrand, Kate. "U.S. Companies Turn to Countertrade in Soviet Union." *Business Marketing* (May 1990): 22–24.

Black, George. "Tactics for the Russian Front." *Business Marketing* 74, no. 1 (January 1989): 42–46.

Gilbert, Nathaniel. "The Case for Countertrade: How Do You Sell Products to Countries that Don't Have the Cash to Pay for Them?" *Across the Board* 29, no. 5 (May 1992): 43–46.

Ring, Mary Ann. "Countertrade Business Opportunities in Russia." *Business America* 114, no. 1 (January 11, 1993): 15–16.

Slutsker, Gary. "Pick Russian Business Partners with Care." *Forbes* 150, no. 1 (July 6, 1992): 46.

Stevens, Mark. "Big Russian Market for Small U.S. Businesses." *Small Business Reports* 15, no. 9 (September 1, 1990): 24–27.

COUNTERTRADE AS AN EXPORT STRATEGY

Matt Schaffer

For countries with limited funds or nonconvertible currencies, countertrade provides an established trading vehicle. The author describes how this strategy can encourage trade between the U. S. and developing markets.

Matt Schaffer is the author of Winning the Countertrade Wares: New Export Strategies for America, published by John Wiley & Sons in 1989. He is President of D.M. Schaffer Corporation of Sandpoint, Idaho and Washington, D.C., an investment banking firm that does countertrade export consulting and merger and acquisition work for larger companies.

The Christmas 1989 revolution in Romania and the U.S. invasion of Panama, when considered together, depict a U.S. dilemma. The United States has more than adequate military power to rescue a potentially troubled regime close to home. Yet, the United States has few economic tools as a government to assist Romania and its Eastern European neighbors now that they are becoming free.

For example, a U.S. trading company could establish barter and counterpurchase agreements with this emerging part of the world. (Romania could buy U.S. products and pay in cash if a company, in advance, agrees to buy its products.)

There is no U.S. Government trading company in the general sense while Japan, West Germany, and other European countries have many such companies in their private sectors.

The United States has also severely cut back on its U.S. export-import bank loans; there are hardly any funds for making bank loans and guarantees to Eastern Europe. These loans might enable these countries to buy U.S. exports to speed their development. In the 1990s, it appears that Japan and Europe are

better positioned than the United States to trade with Eastern Europe, the Soviet Union, and many Third World countries.

With their nonconvertible currencies, Eastern Europe and the Soviet Union, along with many other countries, use various forms of countertrade. The United States has gotten into the countertrade business reluctantly.

The United States pretends that countertrade does not exist, when much of the world trades this way. U.S. companies do a better job, often without the government support that is available in Europe and Japan. A few U.S. companies, such as General Motors, General Electric (GE), Monsanto, Coca-Cola, Pepsico, and Combustion Engineering, have established trading companies or units that use countertrade to increase sales.

Many U.S. companies, however, still do not use countertrade. And when a major transaction is in the works, even the best-prepared U.S. company must turn to a foreign trading company to market the products that are accepted in the countertrade. In its recent $100 million sale of radar equipment to Jordan in exchange for phosphate, Westinghouse relied on the Japanese trading giant Mitsubishi to sell the mineral through its network.

This transaction illustrates the theory behind modern countertrade. It takes the idea that a product can be substituted for money in part of the transaction and adds a crucial idea: the concept of linked trading or mandated reciprocity.

Types of Countertrade

There are several types of countertrade arrangements, including the following:

Counterpurchase. In 1983, Rockwell used the counterpurchase technique to win a hotly contested sale to Zimbabwe of an $8 million printing press. A key element of Rockwell's successful bid was the offer of 100 percent counterpurchase.

Rockwell Trading company offered to buy $8 million of ferrochrome and nickel, knowing that Zimbabwe has these minerals in oversupply. This agreement to purchase or "counterpurchase" the minerals and export them elsewhere was linked to the basic sales agreement calling for Zimbabwe to pay Rockwell cash for the printing press—cash financed with favorable credit from Great Britain's export credit agency, ECGD. Rockwell sourced or produced the press in Great Britain expressly to secure this favorable financing since U.S. Export-Import Bank loans were not available.

U.S.-based Rockwell developed this counterpurchase and financing strategy for a very simple reason. Its French competitor, Harris, had already been awarded the sale, thanks to a heavily subsidized French loan, which required no down payment, a twenty-year repayment, and 4 percent interest. However, Zimbabwe had not signed the contract and promptly rewarded it to Rockwell after receiving the U.S. company's new offer.

Counterpurchase has been picked up more formally by the countries of Eastern Europe and by several countries in Latin America, including Mexico, Venezuela, and Colombia, which makes it national policy. In counterpurchase, the products traded are not a substitution for money but a catalyst for the creation and release of hard currency. Counterpurchase, like countertrade, flourishes where money or hard currency is scarce.

Barter. While pure barter is rare in modern countertrade, barterlike transactions occur very often.

In 1981, GE resorted to this approach when U.S. Eximbank financing was withdrawn after production on a turbine generator for Romania had already begun. Rather than take a loss on start-up costs already committed, GE agreed to accept Romanian chemicals, metals, steel, rebar, and nails on a credit basis as payment over several years. GE founded its own trading company within two years to turn these items into cash and to handle the trade finance arrangements on individual transactions.

Offsets. In 1975, offset became popular among European countries with NATO's purchase of F-16 aircraft from General Dynamics and with the Swiss purchase of Northrop's F-5. A key feature of the F-16 sale was a coproduction agreement, which set up a production facility in the Netherlands for this state-of-the-art fighter plane. The Swiss added to the coproduction idea by convincing Northrop to export manufactured products from Switzerland (mainly machine tools and electronic components).

Today, offset is requested in nearly all major U.S. military exports; it is spreading beyond the military area into such fields as telecommunications and commercial aircraft.

Offset may involve a complex set of commitments requested from the company seeking to win an export sale. In its 1984 sale of 160 F-16s to Turkey, worth $4.2 billion in 1983 dollars, General Dynamics offered an offset package including (1) coproduction, (2) technology transfer, (3) the export of miscellaneous Turkish products (called indirect offsets), and (4) electronic and military components (called direct offsets because they are more directly related to the F-16 program).

Countries often place a higher value on direct rather than indirect offsets because the related exports tend to strengthen their own domestic defense industry. Thus, when Great Britain and France bought the AWACs airborne radar plane from Boeing in the mid-1980s, these countries valued a commitment by the aircraft manufacturer to purchase certain components for the AWACs in the two countries. This commitment was in addition to prized coproduction agreements calling for Boeing's investment in the French and British manufacturers who supplied components for the plane.

By creating an eventual competitor, U.S. companies try to design an offset that does the least damage to their future sales. This issue is vital for deciding how much technology to transfer.

A U.S. company might bet that technology transferred today will become outmoded in two or three years and, therefore, may not be a threat. The Japanese place great emphasis on technology transfer, stressing it more than any other aspect of the offset concept. In several recent military sales, the Japanese have been aggressive and skillful in extracting a transfer of technology or at least access to it. A succession of military sales to Japan has become increasingly controversial, including Sidewinder missiles from Raytheon, Aegis destroyers from RCA, and FSX planes from General Dynamics (a modified version of the F-16).

The Aegis and FSX were the subject of bitter disputes in Congress during 1988 and 1989 when critics expressed dismay over the large Japanese content in each system and the implications of technology transfer. The companies argued that some sale was better than no sale and that offering a buyer domestic content and access to technology is an accepted marketing technique.

Critics in Congress complained that the United States is simply frittering away its technological advantage and speeding Japan toward its expressed goal of becoming a major exporter of military systems. Japan, they argued, could act more forcefully to reduce the trade deficit by purchasing larger military items "off the shelf" without insisting on the joint venture concept that is so much a part of Japanese business culture and that is central to the notion of offset.

In order to compete, U.S. companies must begin to design offset packages. Japan, South Korea, Australia, Canada (despite the highly touted free-trade agreement), and all European nations have offset policies while the United States does not.

Ideally, no company should negotiate a commitment without a concrete plan for how the commitment will be carried out, even though such precision may not always be possible. Accepting a heavy penalty beyond 3 percent or 4 percent of the unfulfilled offset may be unwise. As with a bank loan, seeking the longest term for carrying out the commitment is often a good idea. Above all, maintaining flexibility for how the offset can be fulfilled is essential. The list of products for export should be as broad as possible, including the right to substitute procurement of components, investment in-country, or the transfer of technology.

General Dynamics has found that investment in-country yields the greatest offset credit for each dollar spent. So far, on a worldwide basis, the company has been able to spend less than $0.04 on average for each $1 of offset credit received.

Coproduction. A key feature of General Dynamics's F-16 sale to Turkey was a coproduction arrangement where the company and its main U.S. subcontractors invested $137 million in an F-16 assembly plant in that country as well as in Turkey's aircraft industry.

Coproduction of this sort, if it can be offered, is becoming a key feature of offsets. For example, in order to sell its twin-jet MD-82 to the Chinese government, McDonnell-Douglas built the first-ever commercial aircraft coproduction factory within the People's Republic. The first airplane in a projected fleet of twenty-five rolled off the assembly line in July 1987.

Compensation. Compensation takes the idea of coproduction one step further. The investing company is repaid with the product of its manufacturing or mining investment while the host government often gives its formal approval and is a partner in the venture.

In the People's Republic of China, where compensation agreements are popular, Occidental Petroleum received a long-term contract to take back ore and refined minerals in return for developing a large mining facility. In Egypt, a major Swiss company, Aluswiss, exports alumina to its newly constructed plant and takes back a portion of the finished aluminum as payment for its investment.

The gradual reduction of trade barriers in the Soviet Union and in the People's Republic of China has spurred countertrade during the past decade. Pepsico has engineered a series of spectacular countertrades with the Soviet Union, trading vodka in the West for soft-drink concentrate over there. More recently, Pepsico agreed to invest in a shipbuilding venture where a portion of the hard currency generated will be used to pay for even more soft-drink sales.

Another factor in the spread of countertrade has been the development of this specialized trade capability within several large U.S. companies in the last ten years, even as Japan and West Germany benefited more naturally from the prior existence of their large general trading companies. Without a Mitsubishi, a Metallgesellschaft, or a national trading network on which to rely, several U.S. corporations have built successful in-house trading companies. Many additional U.S. companies are being slowly drawn into countertrading through third parties or on their own account. The development of this nascent countertrade structure in the United States suggests at least the perception of countertrade as a longer-term trade strategy.

Countertrade in Corporate Strategy

The role of countertrade as both a financial instrument and a sweetener is illustrated by these three transactions:

Ericsson in Uruguay. This 1984 sale of a $90 million telephone switching system to Uruguay helps to explain how countertrade can play a critical role in the formulation of an overall strategy to win a large export.

Ericsson, a Swedish telecommunications firm, triumphed mainly for two reasons. First, the company made the best countertrade offer with a coherent plan to implement it.

Ericsson asked the British investment banking firm Samuel Montague to offer Uruguay 100 percent offset—in other words, a commitment to export $90 million worth of Uruguayan products, including beef, leather goods, and fish. Samuel Montague traded the products through Surinvest, a joint venture trading and financing house co-owned in Montevideo with Uruguayan partners.

A second reason for Ericsson's success was attractive export credit financing. This financing was offered at a bad time for U.S. companies when potentially comparable financing from the U.S. Export-Import Bank had been sharply cut back.

Both Sweden and Brazil, Ericsson's partners, offered a financing package at subsidized rates. The inclusion of Brazil as a major subcontractor was also a clever political tactic, the next best thing to Uruguayan content in the transaction. Brazil was able to exert more political pressure on neighboring Uruguay than would have been possible from a European country acting on its own.

Westinghouse in Jordan. Westinghouse devised an equally effective strategy for winning a $100 million air defense radar system. The Pentagon's foreign military sales funds were not available, yet Jordan still wanted to purchase the radar. Commercial bank terms were unacceptable. In the absence of adequate financing, Westinghouse asked Mitsubishi's trading company to sell the phosphate that Jordan was prepared to offer as a form of payment.

The prime contractor was Lor-West of Bermuda, 20 percent owned by Westinghouse and 80 percent owned by Lorad, a subsidiary of Wraxall Group in the United Kingdom. Westinghouse Defense was a subcontractor to Lor-West.

Between June 1985 and December 1987, Mitsubishi was able to sell $70 million in phosphate rock through its worldwide trading network, ahead of the delivery schedule for the radar. The foreign exchange proceeds for the sale were remitted from Mitsubishi back to a special account in the central bank of Jordan.

To establish viable and secure payment procedures, separate contracts were set up between Lor-West and Mitsubishi, Mitsubishi and the central bank, and Lor-West and the central bank. The central bank issued an unconfirmed letter of credit to Lor-West.

As payments for the air defense system were required, they were automatically drawn through the letter of credit out of an escrow account in Chase Manhattan Bank of the United Kingdom's Channel Islands. This offshore payment mechanism, outside either the buying or selling country, provided additional assurance to Lor-West and Westinghouse that funds would be transferred smoothly as the delivery for the radar was met.

N-Ren in Madagascar. The problems that N-Ren International faced and overcame with countertrade are the stuff of legend.

N-Ren, a small engineering and construction firm based in Brussels, began building a $60 million fertilizer plant in 1979. By 1983, Madagascar ran out of money to pay for the plant, even though the plant was 95 percent complete and 98 percent of the equipment was delivered. The delayed payments created cost overruns and drove up the price of finishing the plant.

Tom Snyder, the U.S. president of N-Ren, personally traveled several times to Tananarive, the capital of Madagascar, trying to resolve the impasse—all to no avail. Finally, when the situation seemed hopeless, a breakthrough occurred. Madagascar proposed to pay for the plant's completion with cloves, a spice for which the country is famous. Snyder obtained approvals from the Ministries of Finance and Agriculture, The Revolutionary Council (or cabinet of ministers), and ultimately President Didier Ransiraka.

Fortunately, the government of Madagascar already had direct and convenient access to the cloves, routinely buying the spice from twelve private sector buyers with local currency (the Malgache franc). Depending on the country, it is not always so easy for the government to buy commodities with local currency. The Malgache franc was also tied to the French franc, giving it a stabler value.

Between 1983 and 1988, four shipments of cloves took place in order to generate hard currency funds for the completion of the factory. The ships docked and took the cloves at Tamatave, the port where the fertilizer factory was also located. The ships then sailed for Rotterdam, the port where Catz International, one of the world's foremost spice trading companies and N-Ren's partner, was established.

The first two shipments were valued at approximately $10 million each (1,200 tons for the first shipment and 2,000 tons for the next one, as the world's cloves price continued to fall).

For each shipment, numerous technical problems were overcome. N-Ren took out Lloyd's insurance through a Belgian agent. A shipping agent in Hamburg, West Germany, arranged transportation space on a suitable ship. The general manager of the fertilizer plant was at dockside to inspect every 50 kilo bag loaded on board. For each bag, there were about eight to ten documents concerning such issues as weight, origin, quality, and health factors. Nonconforming bags were rejected at dockside. The cloves were sold against documents called bills of lading, whose physical transfer signified the passing of title.

As savvy traders, Catz made N-Ren take title to a portion of the cloves at Tamatave, knowing the price would have fallen further by the time a ship reached port in Rotterdam and offering the prospect of a greater profit on resale. Catz guaranteed payment to N-Ren for the rest of the cloves at a fixed price.

To support this guarantee to N-Ren, Catz opened up a letter of credit with its bank, Credit Anstalt, in London. The letter of credit was confirmed by the American Express bank in Hamburg. Once the ship arrived in Rotterdam, documents were presented to Credit Anstalt; it immediately paid N-Ren under the letter of credit.

In one shipment, the captain persisted in unloading the cloves during violent rainstorms in Rotterdam, despite pleas from N-Ren executives and even though it is well-known that water can damage cloves. He claimed that he was under pressure to meet another contracted shipping schedule and could not wait for a change in the weather.

Catz's bonded warehouse salvaged much of this shipment of cloves by bringing in a specialized kiln company to dry the spice, allowing the bags to be repackaged. A year-long dispute finally resulted in an insurance settlement of several hundred thousand dollars for the damaged portion of the cloves.

In another transfer of the spice, N-Ren's general counsel found that the ship actually vanished for several days. He finally tracked it down in a small port north of Lisbon. Use of the vessel's time had come under legal dispute. N-Ren and French, Swiss, and West German companies with cargo on board all had to make a payment of tribute to the vessel's owner to get the ship's time released. As the fourth and final shipment came to a close, Snyder and the government of Madagascar were hopeful that the proceeds would give the completed plant operating capital during its early years of production.

N-Ren learned many lessons from its experience, aside from the fact that small companies can also do countertrade. The company wisely insisted that local weights govern the transaction since cloves take on weight and water by up to 3 percent in a tropical climate and lose weight in a drier climate. The falling price of cloves over the five-year period created another favorable precondition since, in a strong market, the government would not likely have offered the spice.

Developing a relationship with Catz International was essential, especially for the first two or three shipments because of N-Ren's initial lack of trading experience. Careful attention was paid to all the documentation, which helped during the insurance proceedings related to the one partially damaged shipment. Snyder and his colleagues meticulously monitored the transaction all the way through and resourcefully solved problems each time that they surfaced. Above all, in the crucial early stages, Snyder succeeded in developing a personal relationship with key government officials that helped expedite the transaction.

As this and the previous examples illustrate, countertrade is a way of doing business and thinking about business that raises the almost tribal concept of reciprocity to a new level of importance. The relationship between trading partners is critical, taking on ever greater importance as less cash for products is available and as more barter takes place.

NEW TRENDS IN COUNTERTRADE

Margitta Wülker-Mirbach

'Countertrade' as traditionally understood, is the exchange of goods for goods—a kind of international barter. It has long been a feature in world trade and is mainly used in order to finance imports and promote exports.[1] But there are grounds for objection, among them that:

■ compensation deals accentuate bilateralism and thus run counter to the spirit of the open and multilateral system of international trade, as embodied in the General Agreement on Tariffs and Trade.

■ countertrade practices tend to hinder structural adjustment in the countries which resort to them—and structural adjustment is frequently stipulated by the IMF as a condition for further lending.

Countertrade practices were long associated primarily with East-West trade. They spread to North-South and South-South trade only in the early 1980s. Countertrade increased until the mid-1980s, especially since the oil-producing nations insisted on using oil in countertrade when buying other goods from consuming nations. (For 1983, the OECD estimated countertrade at a maximum of approximately

Reprinted from Margitta Wülker-Mirbach, "New Trends in Countertrade," *The OECD Observer*, April/May 1990:/63.

Margitta Wülker-Mirbach is a specialist in countertrade in the OECD Trade Directorate.

[1] For the advantages and disadvantages of countertrade, see Jacques de Miramon, 'Countertrade: A Modernized Barter System', *The OECD Observer*, No. 114, January 1982: and for the interest of developing countries in countertrade, see Jacques de Miramon, 'Countertrade: An Illusory Solution', *The OECD Observer*, No. 134, May 1985.

[2] *Countertrade: Developing Country Practices*, OECD Publications, Paris, 1985.

4.8% of world trade.[2]) That increase seems to have been followed by relative calm. Nevertheless, some of the characteristics of countertrade have since changed, especially to the extent that countertrade seems to have become an important element of industrialisation policy. Several interesting tendencies can be observed.

The New Phenomenon of 'Offsets'

Although the more traditional form of 'commercial compensation' (goods against goods) still occurs on a much larger scale, 'industrial compensation' (goods against investment) has grown in importance. Industrial compensation takes the form either of 'buy-backs' (repayment in products derived from the original sale, frequently in connection with the sale of an industrial or mining plant) or of 'offsets'.

Buy-backs have been known for longer in countertrade deals. They involve longer-term agreements which may have the advantage over one-off deals of ensuring that market links are continued. One well-known buy-back deal was the delivery of gas pipelines by the German company Mannesmann to the Soviet Union in the 1970s for gas from Siberia.

The second form of industrial compensation, the 'offset', can be broadly defined as arrangements under which foreign suppliers implement specific actions aimed at partially or fully compensating (off-setting) the buyer's procurement costs by making investments in the client country in plant, component or related industries, by co-producing, by giving commissions to sub-contractors, and so on.

Offsets attracted widespread attention in the press and in public debate only two years ago, mainly because of the supposed delays in the implementation of offset commitments of Boeing under a contract to supply its AWACS airborne radar system to the UK Ministry of Defence. Boeing had promised to buy British goods worth 130% of the value of the AWACS sale—which in turn, according to the joint announcement made by the Ministry and Boeing, meant jobs in Britain.

Traditionally, offsets were applied only to government purchases of aeronautical and military equipment, especially in trade among developed countries. More recently, offsets appear to have been increasingly applied in trade, especially with developing countries, and now include civil projects. Early in 1989, for instance, an offset arrangement was made between Tunisia and automobile manufacturers in several developed countries. The manufacturers, including Peugeot and Volkswagen, agreed to purchase Tunisian-made electronic and mechanical components covering half the cost of the imported vehicles.

As part of a £1 billion economic offset programme linked to UK defence sales to Saudi Arabia, British Aerospace proposed, as a joint venture, an aluminium smelter that could export supplies to Britain. And to sell helicopters to South Korea, with a value of $250m, Bell Helicopters had to confer sub-contracts of $125m on the Korean companies Samsung and Daewoo since Korea requires a 50% offset in arms sales.

As these examples show, industrial compensation (buy-backs and offsets), unlike commercial compensation (goods against goods), entails long- rather than short-term arrangements, frequently with a high value per transaction. They are thus not an *ad hoc* phenomenon. Developing countries consider offsets, as well as buy-backs, as a vehicle for more rapid industrialisation.

The drive for modernisation, indeed, explains the current focus of Eastern European countries on joint ventures. In 1989, for example, two consortia of French companies were formed, both backed by Credit Lyonnais, one to promote countertrade (apparently mainly in the form of commercial compensation), the other to promote joint ventures with the Soviet Union. Joint ventures frequently contain a buy-back element.

Development of South-South Trade

South-south countertrade has grown considerably over the last years. Bilateral payments and clearing arrangements have been concluded—between countries of the South and Comecon members, as well—and countertrade agreements have been negotiated.[3] Brazil and Iraq, for example, signed a countertrade

protocol in December 1987 that called for $1.2bn of Brazilian exports a year, to be paid half in oil and half in hard currency. Under the December protocol, Brazilian companies were to ship $600m of manufactures a year to Baghdad and Volkswagen to ship a further $600m of parts and cars every year from its São Paulo factories.

There appears to be a lot of countertrade involving Asian countries, especially Indonesia, China, India and Malaysia,[4] not only south-south but also, of course, north-south. Singapore, although not offering countertrade deals as such, seems to be establishing itself as a regional centre for countertrade companies who seek to do business with the Far East (as is Vienna for countertrade with Eastern Europe). To promote the establishment of countertrade service companies, the Singapore Trade Development Board issued guidelines in July 1986, under which, for example, a tax holiday period of five years is given to a company setting up a countertrade subsidiary.

This specialisation, combined with the uncertainty surrounding Hong Kong's future after the transition to Chinese sovereignty in 1997 and Singapore's strategic geographical location and well-developed communications with the Far East and Asia, may be winning large volumes of countertrade from Hong Kong.

There is little countertrade reported from sub-Saharan African countries. Among OPEC countries—virtually all their countertrade exports involve crude oil—Iran, Iraq, Libya and Saudi Arabia are the leading countertraders.

In Latin America, Brazil is the most active countertrader. Yet it has no legislation to promote countertrade, and officially the government opposes mandated countertrade. Other countries, such as Argentina, have comprehensive countertrade legislation, but it is rarely applied.

The Move to Manufactures

In trade with and among developing countries, there is a clear increase in proposals by developing coun-

---

[3] See the lists in *Countertrade Regulations in Selected Developing Countries*, UNCTAD, Geneva, 1989.

[4] *Third World Countertrade*, Produce Studies, Newbury (UK), 1988.

tries to export manufactured goods, although commodities are still the most countertraded products.

Countertrade with developing countries originally involved mostly the exchange of commodities for manufactured goods, on the grounds that virtually every important commodity market—especially for many 'soft' commodities like cocoa and sugar—suffered from a mixture of low prices, stagnant markets and overproduction. It provided a fertile breeding ground for a deviation, through countertrade, from the multilateral trading system.

Most of the countertraded exports of manufactured goods come from developing countries that are more technologically advanced; they seem to be turning to new industrial products for which they lack the international marketing expertise. As part of a deal with Indonesia involving a $337m sale of F16 aircraft, for example, the US firm General Dynamics undertook to market in the United States transport planes which are produced in Indonesia under a joint venture with Spain, to a value of $168m.

The increased role of manufactures in countertrade reflects a global tendency in world trade. In addition, an increasing number of developing countries, especially Hong Kong, Singapore, the Republic of Korea, Taiwan, Malaysia and Thailand (the 'Dynamic Asian Economies' (DAEs)), have emerged as major exporters of such goods. But it would be rash to suggest any specific causal link between the increase of exports of manufactured goods with countertrade. With the exception of Malaysia, these countries are generally little involved in countertrade.

Crude, Cartels and Countertrade

Countertrade with crude oil emerged on a significant scale in the early 1980s, as producers used it as a form of price-discounting in a bid to maintain their market shares when the OPEC cartel reduced the production of crude oil. For some producers, therefore, countertrade was a convenient way of selling more oil at a lower price, thus sidestepping the quota. And crude oil remains the most countertraded product, although there now seem to be fewer transactions than in the mid-1980s, especially compared to countertrade deals with other commodities and manufactured goods.

Beginning in 1986, there was a marked drop in the volume of oil 'sold' in such transactions, for three reason. First, when OPEC effectively abandoned official selling rates at the end of 1985 countertrade no longer offered the advantage of avoiding the quota or keeping prices secret. Second, countertrade deals had already become riskier for Western companies because of the heightened chance of a fall in market prices between agreement and delivery; purchasers were having doubts about disposal, particularly of large quantities for the short term. And third, with the fall in prices for crude oil—because of massive overproduction, at a time when markets were shrinking and trends in the West were towards energy conservation and the exploitation of alternative energy sources—the value of countertrade involving crude oil has fallen, too.

But the indebtedness of developing countries seems to have created a new role for oil countertrade. Exporters to poorer oil producers are starting to recognise the value of oil as an alternative currency, and there seems to be a tendency for countertrade deals in oil to be initiated by the exporters of the developed countries rather than by the developing country. Since foreign exporters, for example, aware of Nigeria's balance of payments difficulties, were looking for more secure means of payment, Nigeria decided to increase the scope of its oil countertrade to finance general imports. And this although Nigeria, which had been engaged in oil-for-goods swaps on a major scale in 1984–85, had seemed unlikely to resume in countertrade after suffering heavy losses.

Countertrade for Debt Repayment

Countertrade is believed to be used frequently to circumvent debt-servicing obligations. Agreements with creditors often stipulate that a specified portion of hard-currency reserves must be earmarked for the servicing of debt. A country may thus attempt to elude this obligation through countertrade which is not registered in the books of the central bank.

But occasionally countertrade has also been used to pay back the national debt. In October 1987 Midland Bank, Peru's second largest creditor, agreed to sell $22m worth of Peruvian goods, keeping $8.8m as debt repayment and giving the $13.2m remainder to Peru. Midland was supposed to sell some thirty kinds of Peruvian product, including $3.5m worth of iron pellets, $3.5m of fishmeal, $3.1m of steel balls, $3m of coffee, $3m of copper wire and lesser amounts of other goods. Following Midland, First Interstate Bank of California signed a similar contract in Washington for $42m worth of goods, $14m being debt repayment. First Interstate was supposed to sell fewer mineral products and commodities and more agricultural and manufactured goods. Though modest, the two deals constitute Peru's most significant payment to commercial banks for three years.

The experience of Peru with its goods for debt programme was carefully followed by other countries. In 1989, Iraq paid DM400m out of DM1.4 billion debt to the Federal Republic of Germany by means of an oil barter deal with Veba.

This way of paying back debt, of course, favours one creditor over others.

The resorting of a number of countries to countertrade reflects their serious financial and trade difficulties. Yet countertrade is seldom a satisfactory means of solving these problems lastingly and efficiently. At present, countertrade continues to hover at the margin of the multilateral trading system. But governments should be alert towards new developments in countertrade lest it undermine the multilateral trading system in the future.

CASE STUDY: AMERICAN MANAGER IN AN AUSTRALIAN COMPANY

"United Flight 2020 to Honolulu and Los Angeles is now boarding. Please have your tickets and boarding passes ready for the attendant at the gate."

Bob Underwood picked up his briefcase and started toward the jetway. He paused momentarily to look around the passenger waiting area and, as had been the case so often here in Sydney, he saw nothing to indicate that he was in a foreign country. Certainly the accents were different than in the United States, but the language was English and readily understandable. This superficial familiarity, he concluded, was one of the main reasons he had had such a difficult time adjusting to his job at MedScope, Ltd., in Australia.

MedScope was one of three foreign subsidiaries owned by the parent company, MedicoSupplies, Inc. whose headquarters were in Houston, Texas. Bob was on a two-year assignment at MedScope after working in the management information systems (MIS) department in Houston for five years.

As he settled back in his seat on the plane, Bob thought back to the day he arrived in Sydney almost eight months ago. Bob and his family had left Houston on a hot, humid July day and arrived 30 hours later to find Sydney in the middle of winter. That juxtaposition of seasons probably should have alerted him that there would be many differences between the United States and Australia. Instead, during the taxi ride to their hotel through Sydney's modern buildings, everyone seemed to have the impression that they had simply arrived in a different U.S. city.

Bob's boss at MedicoSupplies had encouraged Bob to apply for the position of MIS director in Sydney. Pete Jacobs thought that this international experience would enhance Bob's chances for promotion at MedicoSupplies since he would then have knowledge of a subsidiary's operations. Reluctantly, Bob applied for and obtained the Sydney position. His wife and children had not been enthusiastic about the move to Australia. Bob's daughter, Sara, was in the seventh grade and loved her school; his son, Jim, was in the fifth grade and just had earned the pitcher's spot on his Little League team; and Bob's wife, Marie, worked part-time as a medical technician. After several long family discussions, Bob convinced Marie and the children that this move was extremely important to his career.

During the first few weeks at the Sydney office, everything seemed to go well. Bob met with his new staff during the first week and asked for their help in orienting him to the Australian operations. In this meeting, he outlined his background and industry experience, described his goals for the two years he would be managing the Australian MIS department, and assured them that he had an open door policy and was always available to talk with them on an individual basis.

"I'm looking forward to your working with me to accomplish the company's goals for Australia," he concluded. "Thank you for meeting with me today."

Bob's family had more difficulty making the transition to living in a foreign country. When they first arrived in Sydney, the family lived in a hotel apartment for three weeks while they searched for a house. When they leased a comfortable house in a Sydney suburb similar to their Houston house, Marie spent several days visiting schools and looking for the right one for Sara and Jim. Although there were state-supported schools in their neighborhood, a friend in the United States who had lived in Australia several years ago advised Bob and Marie to find a private school for the children. Deciding on schools and sorting out the equivalent grade levels and subjects proved more difficult than Marie expected, and she asked Bob to spend some time with her talking with school headmasters. Although Bob always had been closely involved in decisions regarding the children, he was reluctant to take time away from the office at the beginning of his tenure in Sydney and left these decisions to Marie.

Colleagues at MedScope organized a welcoming party for the family soon after their arrival, and Bob's boss's wife invited Marie to lunch and the theater. The family had no permanent social group at first, however, and activities that they had enjoyed in Houston were less readily available in their new city. Jim, in particular, missed his Little League team and asked once if he could go back to Houston and live with his grandmother. Bob decided to be patient and hope that Marie and the children would adjust to their new situation after a few weeks.

Over the next six months, Bob stayed very busy learning the Australian company's MIS operations and looking for ways to improve them. Before he left Houston, the MedicoSupplies vice-president of operations, Jason Blanchard, had met with Bob to discuss his assignment in Australia. Jason had made it clear that he believed MIS is a technical area and that it can and should be uniform throughout the company's subsidiaries.

"What we need to do," Jason had said, "is find the most efficient and productive methods, and then put those in place in MedicoSupplies companies, wherever they are located."

Bob's only experience in MIS was in the MedicoSupplies U.S. headquarters office and with a similar company in Dallas. His models, then, for his new assignment were U.S.

models, and when he got to Sydney, he began looking for similarities and differences between the U.S. and Australian operations.

One thing Bob noted immediately was that there were fewer management levels among employees in Australia; in fact, the organizational hierarchy was remarkably flat compared to the U.S. structure. Bob found himself responding to requests and receiving information from technicians as well as managers, and from supervisors as well as heads of departments. At one staff meeting to examine the workflow design in the department, several technicians attended with their managers and participated fully in the discussions. When Bob asked one of the managers after the meeting if this was a standard procedure, the Australian manager assured him that it was.

"No one knows more about workflow design than Rob and the other technicians," the manager said. "We wouldn't have made as much progress as we did if they hadn't been involved in today's meeting. And we certainly want their support for any changes we might decide to make."

While Bob understood the manager's reasoning, he was uncomfortable having so many people involved in what he regarded as sensitive management discussions. When the same topic appeared on the meeting agenda later that month, he asked specifically that only designated managers attend. And to keep the meeting within a reasonable time frame, Bob limited the discussion on each point to 10 minutes. When this second meeting was over, he felt that much more had been accomplished with fewer participants and in less time.

About three months after arriving in Australia, Bob's boss, Emily Zortan, the general manager of MedScope, asked Bob what decision the MIS department had made regarding new software and equipment for the sales department. Bob's predecessor had amassed several files of material and information from numerous suppliers, and he had secured bids from five companies for the purchase. After reviewing the files and the bids, Bob recommended the Trujex Company in Hong Kong. Their bid was lower than three of the other companies', they promised a shorter delivery time, and Bob knew something about their product from conversations with managers in the U.S. and London offices of MedicoSupplies.

Later that month, Frank Ricardo, one of the systems analysts in Bob's department, came to Bob's office and asked if he had time to discuss a pending purchase for one of the company's departments.

"If you mean the purchase of a new system for sales," Bob said, "I've already taken care of that. Emily asked for my recommendation a few weeks ago and I told her we'd go with Trujex."

"But you didn't ask me or any of the other analysts which system we would recommend," replied Frank.

"Well, no, but I had all of the information I needed in Preston's files. He had bids from five companies, plus a mountain of information on seven or eight companies. Surely you and the other analysts gathered that data for him, or at least recommended the companies to contact."

"Yes, we did," Frank said. "But we hadn't finished discussing the advantages and disadvantages of each system, nor had all the technicians given their opinions. Preston was planning to meet with us several times before giving Emily the department's decision."

"I think I had all the information I needed," Bob stated, with a note of finality in his voice. "I reviewed the files thoroughly and recommended Trujex based on sound reasons. I'm sorry you and the others didn't have the opportunity to discuss it further, but I felt that a timely decision was what Emily wanted."

As Frank left his office visibly upset, Bob wondered again how Preston had accomplished anything if he had held frequent meetings with all or many of his staff members to go over seemingly straightforward procedures and decisions.

In an effort to decrease his span of control, and to achieve Jason Blanchard's objective of putting the most productive and efficient methods in place, Bob worked for the next several weeks on a reorganization plan for MedScope's MIS operations. As soon as he thought he had a good understanding of the company as a whole and of the specific functions of the MIS department, Bob put together a plan that encouraged specialization among the department's employees. He divided the group in four, assigning each of the four groups to one of the company's functional areas: administration, finance, research, and marketing. Under this scheme, each of the four groups would concentrate on the MIS needs of its designated functional area and thus become more proficient in serving that group of users. Moreover, fewer managers would report directly to Bob as head of the department and he would have more time to devote to planning.

When Bob finished the reorganization plan, he called his top managers to a staff meeting.

"The purpose of our staff meeting today," Bob began, "is to discuss an opportunity for all members of this department to hone their skills by specializing more than they are doing now. I've seen this type of plan work in other companies similar to MedScope and I think you'll agree it has some distinct advantages over the present arrangement."

He passed out copies of the new organizational scheme and spent the next 20 minutes explaining his rationale for the plan. Bob also explained that this was still in the draft stage and that he welcomed ideas from the group on refinements and changes. Finally, he asked the managers for their comments and reactions. No one said anything.

After a few minutes of uncomfortable silence, Bob said, "I'm sure you'll want to take this plan back to your offices and give it some thought. And perhaps discuss it with some of your key people. Why don't you take a couple of days to look at it and then call or memo me with your suggestions."

Two days later, Emily Zortan called Bob to her office for a meeting. She began by saying that several people from Bob's department had called to ask her for letters of recommendation because they were applying for positions in other companies. Emily was anxious to know what Bob thought the problem might be.

"This has never happened before," Emily explained. "I've never had several people come to me with this sort of request. People leave MedScope, of course, to take better jobs somewhere else. But this is too many people all at once. What do you think is going on, Bob?"

"I don't really know," Bob said. "Actually, I'm astonished. No one has complained to me or given any indication that there's a problem. I'm pretty good about recognizing dissatisfaction among my employees, or anticipating problems which may occur. But I haven't seen any evidence of that here."

"How well do you know your employees, Bob?" Emily asked. "I realize you've only been here for eight months and that you've been busy settling in at work and at home. But have you joined them for their Friday get-togethers after work, or gone with them on some of their Saturday excursions? Preston was always talking about what a tight-knit group the MIS department is and how many social activities they organize."

"I did go out with some of them after work a couple of times," Bob replied, "but I have been pretty busy helping Marie and the children adjust to our new situation. And I've always found that it's a good policy to maintain a certain amount of distance from one's employees."

"Oh, there is one thing that I know might be a source of irritation. Jack Strath mentioned that he had requested three weeks vacation time for a trip to Bangkok and Singapore, and that you had asked him to take only two weeks instead. Any reason for asking him to cut his trip short?" Emily asked.

"Yes," Bob explained, "I thought that three weeks is too long a time for a key manager to be away. He's working on several critical projects that need to be completed in the next three or four months."

"If I recall correctly," Emily said, "Jack has an excellent assistant who could take over in his absence. That would be good experience for a mid-level manager, don't you think?"

"I suppose so," Bob conceded, "although it's unusual for a senior manager like Jack to take three weeks off."

Emily looked puzzled. "My suggestion is that you give Jack the three weeks he requested. He's worked extremely hard this year and deserves a respite.

"And whatever the problems with other employees, I'm sure we can work them out," Emily continued. "Maybe there's just a simple misunderstanding here. Probably you and I should have spent more time when you first got here, talking about our management style and philosophy here, and seeing if there might be some differences between Australia and the United States. Why don't you think about this and plan to meet with me after you get back from Houston in a couple of weeks."

"Right, I'll give it some thought and see if I've overlooked something. Perhaps I've stepped on somebody's toes without realizing it. I do have a tendency to get caught up in enthusiasm for projects and forget that others may not share that same enthusiasm."

"Have a good trip to Houston, Bob, and we'll talk when you get back," Emily said as she walked him to the door.

As Bob's plane left the runway at Sydney, he thought back to this conversation with Emily and began to review the events of his last eight months at MedScope. What had he done wrong? He knew he was a good manager; his previous bosses all had given him excellent performance appraisal reviews. They always mentioned his technical expertise, his planning skills, and his department's productivity as evidence of what a good job he was doing. Yet, Emily regarded the potential department turnovers as an indication that something was seriously wrong in his department at MedScope. Bob decided he would talk with Pete Jacobs when he got to Houston and review his activities in Sydney. Maybe Pete would be able to help him see where he had made some mistakes.

Instructions:

After carefully reading this case study, answer the following questions:

1. What do you think are the reasons several employees suddenly want to leave Bob's department? What has Bob done during his eight months at MedScope that may have contributed to these employees' dissatisfaction? Are there any cultural differences between the United States and Australia that might explain the problems Bob seems to be having?

2. What could the parent company, MedicoSupplies, have done to prepare Bob and his family for this international assignment? Outline an action plan companies might use in order to increase chances for success among their expatriate managers. Include suggestions for both the manager and members of the manager's family.

3. Articulate and evaluate your own opinion about the degree of "distance" prevalent between U.S. managers and their staffs. Who is protected by this management style? Are there any adverse organizational impacts resulting from this style?

SUGGESTED READINGS

Knotts, Rose. "Cross-Cultural Management: Transformations and Adaptations." *Business Horizons* (January 1989): 29–33.

Mendenhall, Mark, Edward Dunbar, and Gary Oddou. "Expatriate Selection, Training, and Career-Pathing: A Review and Critique," *Human Resource Management*, 26, no. 3 (1987): 331–345.

Murray, F. T. and Alice Murray. "Global Managers for Global Businesses," *Sloan Management Review*, 27, no. 2 (1986): 75–80.

Tung, Rosalee. "Selection and Training of Personnel for Overseas Assignments," *Columbia Journal of World Business*, 16, no. 1 (1981): 68–78.

———. *The New Expatriates: Managing Human Resources Abroad*. Cambridge, MA: Ballinger, 1988.

APPENDIX

I

WORK VALUES EXERCISE—AMERICAN CULTURE

The objective of this exercise is to give you an opportunity to identify your personal work values and to compare these with your peers' personal work values. Your instructor will give you instructions for completing this worksheet.

INDIVIDUAL WORKSHEET

Listed below are 30 different values which may or may not be important to you. Imagine yourself in a work situation, either in a job you now hold or in your expected career after college. Place a check (✓) in front of those values which you believe are important in this work situation and place an "**X**" in front of those values which you believe are *not* important in this work setting.

After you have completed this task, rank-order the three most important values by placing a "1" next to your highest value, a "2" next to your second highest value, and a "3" next to your third highest value.

Remember: Some of the values that you believe are important in your personal relationships may not be the same as those you believe are important in a work situation.

In a work situation, I believe it is valuable to be

____Active	____Explorative	____Sensitive
____Ambitious	____Good	____Spontaneous
____Aware	____Helpful	____Superior
____Better	____Honest	____Supportive
____Careful	____Influential	____Sure
____Competitive	____Loyal	____Thoughtful
____Considerate	____Open	____Tolerant
____Creative	____Productive	____Trusting
____Critical	____Right	____Unique
____Different	____Risky	____Warm

GLOSSARY

This glossary contains definitions of the unusual terms used in the case studies and exercises, and some of the more common words that have a specific connotation within the context of this book. It also includes words that are commonly used in international business situations.

Note: Many of these words have specific meanings within particular disciplines; these may or may not be the same meanings the words have when used in everyday parlance. The definitions given here are the definitions most commonly used by social scientists.

acculturation—the process by which contacts between different cultural groups lead to the acquisition of new cultural traits by one group, or by both groups, as one or both adopt traits of the other group.

alienation—an individual's feelings of estrangement from a situation, group, or culture.

assimilation—originally, social scientists defined this process as the acquisition by immigrant groups of the traits of American culture; as such, it was viewed as unidimensional with the immigrants giving up most, if not all, of the characteristics of their original culture. Now social scientists tend to view this as a two-way process in which members of the dominant American culture acquire (or assimilate) some of the characteristics of the immigrant group at the same time. (See also *acculturation*.)

attitude—a learned and enduring tendency to perceive or act toward persons or situations in a particular way.

barter—the exchange of goods without the use of money; a common form of countertrade.

behavior—the actions or reactions of persons in specified situations. The acceptable behavior of a person from culture A in a particular situation may differ markedly from the acceptable behavior of a person from culture B in the same situation.

belief system—the pattern of ideas or beliefs that exists in a particular society, culture, or subculture.

chauvinism—a prejudiced belief in the superiority of one's own group.

Chicano, Latino, Hispanic—terms used to describe or refer to persons of Latin American heritage living in the United States.

compadrazgo—used in Spain and Spanish-speaking New World countries to refer to the relationship between a child's parents and godparents. This relationship may have economic, as well as social, dimensions and it may extend to the workplace.

countertrade—the exchange of goods, technology, services, or ideas that involves more than the exchange of money. Examples include trading goods for goods (barter), and trading goods and services for a combination of goods and cash under two separate contracts or agreements to be fulfilled at different times (counterpurchase).

cross-cultural—literally, between cultures. The term is used in this book to designate the comparison of actions or behaviors as a result of contact between individuals from different cultures. (See also *intercultural* and *multicultural*.)

cultural relativism—the tradition that one should judge and interpret aspects of other cultures within the context of those cultures, that is, according to the rules and beliefs of that culture, rather than according to the criteria used in one's own culture.

culture—The classic definition is Edward Tylor's from his *Primitive Culture* (1871): "That complex whole which includes knowledge, belief, art, morals, law, custom, and any other capabilities acquired by man as a member of society."

culture shock—the reaction of a group or individual to a new, unfamiliar cultural environment. This reaction may occur when traveling or living in such an environment, and it often follows a U-shaped pattern. At the top left of the U is the euphoria or excitement a person feels when arriving in a new situation. Gradually, dealing with the unfamiliar on a daily basis becomes overwhelming and the person moves toward the bottom of the U with feelings of loneliness, disorientation, alienation, or mild depression. After a time, as the person gains familiarity with the environment, one moves up the curve toward total, or nearly total, adjustment to the environment.

Interestingly, the person who has been living in a foreign culture may experience a similar reaction when returning to one's own culture; the re-adjustment to one's own culture usually takes less time than the adjustment to the other culture, but often the individual passes through the same stages a second time.

custom—cultural tradition or habitual form of behavior within a given social group. Acting contrary to one of these customs may result in social disapproval or even ostracism.

enculturation—the process by which individuals learn the elements of their own culture.

ethnic group—a group of people who set themselves apart and are set apart from other groups in a society on the basis of race, language, cultural patterns, and so on.

ethnocentrism—the tendency to judge or evaluate other cultures in terms of one's own; often, the belief that one's own culture is superior to all others.

expatriate—a citizen of one country living and/or working in another country. This term is often applied to managers who accept assignments in other countries and to members of their families who accompany the manager abroad.

extended family—a household unit that includes relatives or fictive kin (individuals not related by consanguinity or by marriage but who are regarded in the same manner as related individuals) in addition to parents and children. For example, this may include grandparents, aunts, uncles, and cousins. (See also *nuclear family*.)

founder culture—a term used to refer to the culture of an organization in which the influence of the founder's values, beliefs, and practices are still dominant, regardless of whether the founder is still present in the organization.

heterogeneity—when applied to a specific culture, the term means that that culture is made up of dissimilar and diverse groups.

high context—term used by Edward T. Hall to describe cultures in which individuals share a high degree of common knowledge about many things and thus communicate much information *implicitly*.

homogeneity—when applied to a specific culture the term means that that culture includes similar groups.

individualism—a series of loosely related political, social, and/or historical theories that give the interests of the individual precedence over the interests of the group. One distinction often noted between the United States and Japan is the emphasis Americans place on the individual compared to the emphasis the Japanese give to the group.

intercultural—between cultures; used interchangeably with cross-cultural.

kinship—the complex system of social relationships based on marriage (affinity) and birth (consanguinity).

kiva—a large, rectangular or circular, underground chamber used by Pueblo Indian men for religious ceremonies. The chamber has a fire pit in the center and is accessible by ladder. An opening in the floor of the kiva represents the entrance to the lower world which is believed to be the opening through which life emerged into this world.

low context—a term used by Edward T. Hall to describe cultures in which individuals share a small degree of common knowledge and thus communicate much information *explicitly*.

machismo—a term meaning "maleness"; an attitude held by many Latin American men toward women. It connotes power, virility, competitiveness, and aggressiveness.

melting pot—a term coined to describe the apparent assimilation of immigrant groups into the dominant American culture. In recent years, social scientists and others have begun to question the validity of this concept, pointing to the cultural diversity that characterizes the United States.

monochronic—a term used by Edward T. Hall to describe those cultures in which time is regarded as a commodity; people in these cultures value promptness and adherence to schedules. Examples of monochronic cultures include German, Swiss, and American. (See also *polychronic*.)

mores—behavior patterns that are accepted, traditional, and usually change slowly.

multicultural—consisting of many cultures.

Native Americans/American Indians—the groups of peoples and their descendants who make up the aboriginal peoples of North America.

nonverbal communication—includes gestures, body posture, and facial expressions. International business people need to be aware that the meanings of nonverbal communication patterns vary from one culture to another; a gesture that is socially acceptable in one culture, for example, may have an obscene or derogatory meaning in another.

nuclear family—a household unit that includes two generations, parents and children.

oral tradition—that part of a society's cultural knowledge which is passed on in verbal form rather than in written form.

organizational culture—the unique set of values, beliefs, behaviors, and artifacts that characterizes a particular organization.

patrón—an individual in Spain and Spanish-speaking countries of the New World who watches out for the interests of certain individual(s); the relationship involves a difference in status with the *patrón* having the higher status. The term may refer to the boss or supervisor at work; or, it may be used in a social context to designate a person who has special responsibilities and obligations to another.

polychronic—a term used by Edward T. Hall to describe those cultures that emphasize relationships with people and the completion of current tasks over strict adherence to schedules. Examples of polychronic cultures include most Latin American countries and countries in southern Europe. (See also *monochronic*.)

protocol—the forms of etiquette and ceremony appropriate in specific situations. International business transactions require a knowledge of how these forms vary in different cultures. In a polychronic culture, for example, one usually discusses nonbusiness topics at the beginning of a meeting as a means of establishing rapport.

proxemics—a field of study associated with anthropologist Edward T. Hall that studies the cultural and social use of space by individuals.

pueblo—the communal dwelling of many Indian groups in Arizona and New Mexico. It is made of adobe or stone; individual units are entered by a ladder through an opening in the roof.

repatriation—the process of returning to one's own country after traveling or living in another.

role—any standardized social position with specific rights and obligations; similar to status, but role usually refers to the actions or behaviors expected from an individual with a particular status.

sex (or gender) roles—those activities specifically assigned to males or females in a given culture. In some instances, these roles are rigidly applied; in others, men and women may perform these functions simultaneously or alternately.

socialization—the process by which an individual learns the rules governing the behavior expected from members of one's society. The process includes both formal education and informal instruction from family, peers, and associates.

society—a group of persons living as an entity and having its own culture.

status—any stable position within a society that has specific rights, duties, and expectations attached to it. This may be an ascribed (inherited or earned by membership in a particular group) or an achieved (earned by merit or hard work) position.

stereotype—an image of or an attitude towards a group or a person based on preconceived ideas rather than experience and/or observation.

stratification—a systematic ranking of persons into categories. Examples include the caste system in India and the (formal and informal) class system of many Western cultures.

subculture—a group within a larger society possessing common traits that sets it apart, such as religion or ethnic background.

synergy—the action of two or more entities working together to produce results that neither could produce individually.

taboo—any action that is proscribed by a society, either for pragmatic or symbolic reasons.

technology—the total system by which a human group interacts with its environment, including the use of tools, how it organizes work, the information and knowledge its members use, and the organization of resources for productive activity.

tradition—patterns of beliefs, customs, values, behavior, and knowledge that are passed on from one generation to the next through the socialization or enculturation process.

values—the central beliefs and purposes of an individual or of a society. For example, a widely held value in Japanese corporations is the practice of decision making by consensus.

work ethic—the value an individual or a group ascribes to productive activity. In the United States, for example, the Protestant work ethic has had a strong influence since the colonial period; the main tenet of this ethic is that working hard is a virtue (and, originally, the best way to please God). Other cultures have beliefs regarding work that place less emphasis on the importance of working hard, or that define "hard work" differently than Americans.

worldview (Weltanschauung)—the system of values, attitudes, and beliefs held by a particular group, such as a nation or a subculture. It includes that group's assumptions regarding such things as time, space, nature, society, and self.

APPENDIX

III

FILMS FOR CROSS-CULTURAL STUDIES

The films in this appendix can be used to supplement your understanding of your own or other cultures. Extracting cultural information from some of the films will be very challenging, but all the films are interesting and thought-provoking.

The authors strongly encourage you to use foreign films as an ongoing method for raising awareness of relevant themes and events in other cultures. Consider keeping a notebook in which you record your historical and cultural observations after seeing a film.

These films were produced in and portray a diverse sampling of nations; they include both historical and contemporary studies. Most, but not all, of the films listed here are available on videotape. (Note: The films are listed under the main country depicted in the film, not necessarily the country in which they were produced.)

Algeria
Ramparts of Clay
Argentina
The Official Story
Australia
The Coca-Cola Kid
Malcolm
My Brilliant Career
Silver City
Walkabout
A Woman's Story
Brazil
Bye Bye Brazil

China
Close to Eden (Mongolia)
From Mao to Mozart: Isaac Stern in China
The Horse Thief
Iron and Silk
Ju Dou
Red Sorghum
Denmark
Babette's Feast
Pelle the Conqueror
England
84 Charing Cross Road
My Beautiful Laundrette
France
Au Revoir les Enfants (Good-bye Children)
Murmur of the Heart
Sunday in the Country
Germany
The Marriage of Maria Braun
The Nasty Girl
Wings of Desire
Hong Kong
Boat People
India
Gandhi
The Home and the World
Salaam Bombay
Ireland
Cal
Italy
Bread and Chocolate
Three Brothers

109

Japan

   The Japanese Version

   Kagemusha

   Mr. Baseball

   Rashomon

   Tokyo Story

Mali

   Yeelen (Brightness)

Nigeria

   Yaaba

Poland

   Man of Iron

   Man of Marble

Russia (Soviet Union)

   Freeze, Die, Come to Life

   Moscow Does Not Believe in Tears

   Taxi Blues

Scotland

   Gregory's Girl

   Local Hero

South Africa

   Cry Freedom

   The Gods Must Be Crazy

   A World Apart

United States

   A Midnight Clear

   Chan is Missing

   Dim Sum

   Say Amen, Somebody

   Sherman's March

   To Kill A Mockingbird

Turkey

   Yol

SUGGESTED READINGS

For descriptions of the films listed here and for additional titles, consult one of the following film guides:

Bergan, Ronald, and Robyn Karney. *The Faber Companion to Foreign Films.* Boston: Faber and Faber, 1992.

Huffhines, Kathy Schulz, ed. *Foreign Affairs.* San Francisco: Mercury House, Inc., 1991.

Skorman, Richard. *Off-Hollywood Movies: A Film Lover's Guide.* New York: Harmony Books, 1989.

BIBLIOGRAPHY

Adler, Nancy. *International Dimensions of Organizational Behavior.* 2d ed. Boston: PWS-Kent Publishing, 1991.

Althen, Gary. *American Ways: A Guide for Foreigners in the United States.* Yarmouth, ME: Intercultural Press, 1988.

Axtell, Roger. *Do's and Taboo's of Hosting International Visitors.* New York: John Wiley and Sons, 1990.

Benedict, Ruth. *The Sword and the Chrysanthemum.* Boston: Houghton Mifflin, 1989 (Originally published 1946).

Braganti, Nancy, and Elizabeth Devine. *European Customs and Manners.* Deephaven, MN: Meadowbrook Books, 1984.

Charih, M. *Culture and Management: A Bibliography.* Monticello, IL: Vance Bibliographies, 1991.

Chu, Chin-Ning. *The Asian Mind Game: Unlocking the Hidden Agenda of the Asian Business Culture.* New York: Rawson Associates, 1991.

Condon, John C. *With Respect to the Japanese: A Guide for Americans.* Yarmouth, ME: Intercultural Press, 1984.

Copeland, Lennie, and Lewis Griggs. *Going International: How to Make Friends and Deal Effectively in the Global Marketplace.* New York: Random House, 1984.

Culturgrams. Provo, UT: David M. Kennedy Center for International Studies, Brigham Young University, 1992.

De Mente, Boye. *Chinese Etiquette and Ethics in Business.* Lincolnwood, IL: NTC Business Books, 1989.

De Vita, Philip, and James Armstrong. *Distant Mirrors: America as a Foreign Culture.* Belmont, CA: Wadsworth, 1993.

Devine, Elizabeth, and Nancy Braganti. *Asian Customs and Manners.* New York: St. Martin's Press, 1986.

Engholm, Christopher. *When Business East Meets Business West: The Guide to Practice and Protocol in the Pacific Rim.* New York: John Wiley and Sons, 1991.

Ferraro, Gary. *The Cultural Dimensions of International Business.* Englewood Cliffs: Prentice-Hall, 1990.

Geertz, Clifford. *The Interpretation of Cultures.* New York: Basic Books, 1973.

Graham, John L. and Yoshihiro Sano. *Smart Bargaining: Doing Business with the Japanese.* New York: Harper and Row, 1989.

Hall, Edward T. *The Hidden Dimension.* New York: Doubleday, 1966.

————. *The Silent Language.* New York: Doubleday, 1981.

Hall, Edward T., and Mildred Reed Hall. *Hidden Differences: Doing Business with the Japanese.* New York: Doubleday, 1987.

Hamada, Tomoko. *American Enterprise in Japan.* Albany: State University of New York, 1991.

Harris, Philip R., and Robert T. Moran. *Managing Cultural Differences.* 3d ed. Houston: Gulf Publishing, 1991.

Hofstede, Geert. *Culture's Consequences: International Differences in Work-Related Values.* Newbury Park: Sage Publications, 1984.

Kirpalani, V. H., ed. *International Business Handbook.* New York: Haworth Press, 1990.

Komai, Hiroshi. *Japanese Management Overseas: Experiences in the United States and Thailand.* Tokyo: Asian Productivity Organization, 1989.

Koopman, Albert. *Transcultural Management: How to Unlock Global Resources.* Cambridge, MA: Basil Blackwell, 1991.

Lebra, Takie. *Japanese Patterns of Behavior.* Honolulu: University of Hawaii Press, 1976.

March, Robert M. *The Japanese Negotiator: Subtlety and Strategy Beyond Western Logic.* Tokyo: Kodanasha, 1988.

McCreary, Don. *Japanese-U.S. Business Negotiations: A Cross-Cultural Study.* New York: Praeger Publishers, 1986.

Mead, Richard. *Cross-Cultural Management Communication.* New York: John Wiley and Sons, 1990.

Ricks, David A. *Big Business Blunders: Mistakes in Multinational Marketing.* Homewood, IL: Dow Jones-Irwin, 1983.

Rohlen, Thomas P. *For Harmony and Strength: Japanese White-Collar Organization in Anthropological Perspective.* Berkeley: University of California Press, 1974.

Stewart, Edward C. and Milton J. Bennett. *American Cultural Patterns: A Cross-Cultural Perspective.* Rev. ed. Yarmouth, ME: Intercultural Press, 1991.

Terpstra, Vern, and Kenneth David. *The Cultural Environment of International Business.* 3d ed. Cincinnati: South-Western Publishing, 1991.

Tobin, Joseph J., ed. *Re-Made in Japan: Everyday Life and Consumer Taste in a Changing Society.* New Haven: Yale University Press, 1992.

Zimmerman, Mark. *How to Do Business with the Japanese.* New York: Random House, 1985.